THE
FRENCH
COUNTRY
GARDEN

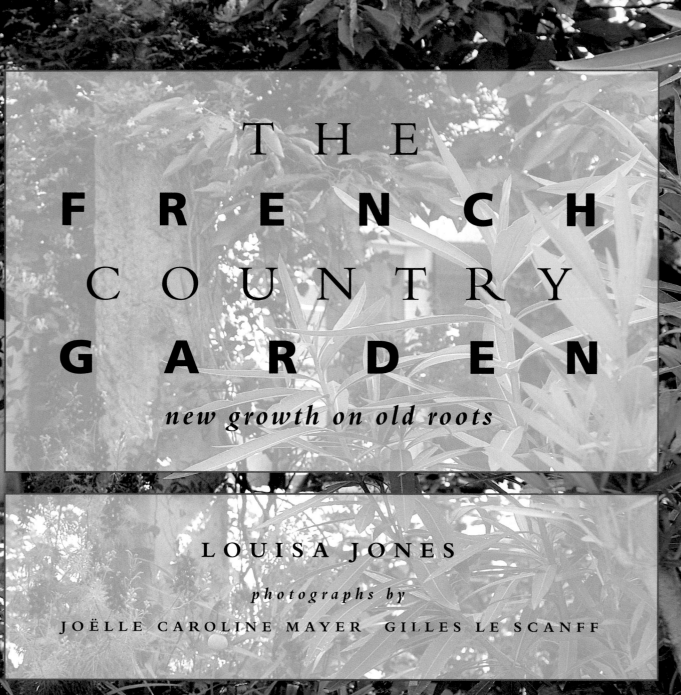

THE FRENCH COUNTRY GARDEN

new growth on old roots

LOUISA JONES

photographs by

JOËLLE CAROLINE MAYER GILLES LE SCANFF

Thames & Hudson

On the title page: The garden of the Bayol family, Saint-Rémy-de-Provence (*see pages 26–33*).

First published in the United Kingdom in 2000 by
Thames & Hudson Ltd, 181A High Holborn,
London WC1V 7QX
www.thamesandhudson.com

First paperback edition 2005

British Library Cataloguing-in-Publication Data
A catalogue record for this book is available from the British Library

ISBN 10: 0-500-28520-9
ISBN-13: 978-0-500-28520-6

Printed and bound in Italy

For all the young people in France today who have made gardening a way of life and a hope for the future.

ACKNOWLEDGMENTS

I would like to thank Parcs et jardins de France for its generous support in the preparation of this book; also the Comités régionaux de tourisme (especially Centre-Val de Loire, Aquitaine, Normandie and Limousin), which helped with my travel expenses in the early stages of the project, when even I did not know exactly what shape it would eventually take. Dozens of garden owners all over France received me very graciously, and I regret that I could not include all of them in the book. Many experts, designers and scholars took time to advise me and to comment on my ideas as they evolved over the last few years, especially Alain Richert, Patrice Fustier and Jean-Paul Pigeat. Leslie Forbes was particularly helpful with the introduction. François Chaslin has for many years made regular contributions to my library, which proved invaluable during my research (although he will never let himself be interviewed!). Annie François has provided the moral support of a sensitive and experienced publisher for every book I have written. The photographers, Gilles Le Scanff and Joëlle Caroline Mayer, have been unfailingly enthusiastic, reliable and, above all, very talented. Special thanks go to the whole team at Thames & Hudson, from the warehouse packers to the senior editors, with whom it has been a great privilege to work. But the person who has proven to be the most constant, helpful and sympathetically critical throughout the years is my husband, to whom I owe the greatest thanks.

Louisa Jones

We wish to express our most sincere gratitude to all the garden owners and gardeners who, by opening the gates of their gardens to us, made the photography in this book possible.

Joëlle Caroline Mayer and Gilles Le Scanff

CONTENTS

3 CELEBRATION OF THE SENSES 66

'Gardens for the five senses' have multiplied all over France in recent years. Inspired often by the careful designs of the Middle Ages and the Renaissance, or by ornamental potagers, these gardens provide fragrance, flavour and texture, as well as good looks. Sensuous awakening has become a favourite concern in public plantings, while private versions offer new variations on the pleasure garden.

5 NATURE'S WAYS 120

In this country of four hundred regional cheeses, good living has always been linked to spirit of place. Ecologically aware gardens inspired by French country landscapes maintain this tradition. Protecting local ecosystems and economizing natural resources, such gardens also enjoy playing with nature, so that 'natural' or 'wild' gardening moves easily towards art.

4 FORMAL PLAY 94

The classical parterre persists in French gardens, but now it has become witty and subversive. Green geometries play with nature rather than dominate it, becoming labyrinths, topiary adventures, sculpture and land art. Formal gardens today explode into new colours and textures with wood fencing and live hedging, flower patterns and field designs.

6 PLANETARY PERSPECTIVES 146

French gardeners participate more and more in worldwide exchanges of knowledge, plants and resources, while sharing general concern for wiser management of our threatened planet. With the fast-spreading fashion for 'green tourism', professional designers create original public sites where visitors experience new links between local and global perspectives.

PREFACE

Gardens today are moving ahead, by leaps and bounds. Only ten years ago, when I was consulted on the Palais Royal gardens in Paris, I was asked not to make waves: the controversial sculptures of Daniel Buren had left a bad taste in the mouths of the politicians. And yet, without drawing attention to ourselves, we managed to change the character of the gardens completely, for the greater pleasure of all concerned. In fact, Parisians proved themselves to be ready for innovation, as they have continued to do, calling for new parks, plant shows and exhibitions. Nor have the provinces lagged behind. Little by little, the traditional sedate country style has given way to more modern conceptions, social consciousness and technical innovation. So much so that the good old profession of garden designer has taken some knocks. Today, creative originality and generosity spring less from large public projects than from those apparently trivial places called gardens. The return to gardening is not just a fashion but a deep social change. It is not merely a compensation for the stresses of our times, still less an expression of nostalgia for the pretty and reassuring scenes we see on calendars.

Louisa Jones, who has lived in France for thirty years, has seen it all happen. She has observed and noted our evolution with sympathy and understanding in her many books on French gardens. So have Gilles Le Scanff and Joëlle Mayer, whose watchful eyes catch better than anyone else's the garden's intimate details. Their book shows perfectly that the garden today is a place where everyone has fun, is creative without pretension, exchanges information, experiments freely, and accepts the diversity of ideas and lessons learnt from experience.

And also that the important gardens today are not always made by professionals …

Jean-Paul Pigeat
Director, Conservatoire international des parcs
et jardins et du paysage de Chaumont-sur-Loire
December 1999

NEW GROWTH ON OLD ROOTS

The green wave

Gardening has become a national passion in France. The great French garden heritage still thrives: classic parterres and landscaped parks continue to flourish alongside botanical collections and family kitchen gardens. But in recent years there has been luxuriant new growth on the old roots. The most remarkable dimension of this renaissance is also its most secret: the home gardens hidden in remote provinces, often made with limited means, but always displaying personal resourcefulness and creativity. This book is mainly about them.

Attitudes towards gardening in France have changed radically, sometimes in ways that echo international trends. But French gardeners have now stopped imitating foreign models, especially the English mixed borders that the horticultural press displayed so lavishly in the 1970s and '80s. The home garden is no longer simply a refined complement to the house, a pretty décor or a leisure activity for weekend relaxation. It has become a place in which to experience a renewed sense of partnership with nature, to welcome wildlife and preserve biodiversity, to rediscover the scents, textures and flavours of the living world, to

combine economy with beauty, to tell a story, to invent personal symbols and to create art. For many, the home garden offers the quintessence of good country living. But what does this mean today?

'French country'

Geographically, France is perhaps the most diverse country in Europe. Stretching from the Mediterranean in the south to the lowlands of the north, and from the Alps in the east to the Atlantic in the west, it encompasses areas with Flemish, Celtic, Germanic, Italian and Hispanic roots. Each of these regions has kept its own unique identity and culture. Good living in France has always been linked to this unusual variety. Jean Cabanel, for ten years director of the influential Mission du Paysage, notes that the French countryside changes its character roughly every thirty kilometres. He estimates, in fact, that France (a country smaller than Texas) has roughly six hundred distinct physical and cultural landscapes. This figure echoes France's boasts of having six hundred wines and four hundred cheeses, all themselves linked to a place of origin, often with the prestigious *appellation d'origine controllé* (AOC – controlled origin) label, which now identifies not only wines and cheeses but green lentils, olive oils and many other products. Thirty years ago, French gardening magazines never located their examples by region, but any current article's opening words now situate the garden precisely. 'Spirit of place' not only provides clues for climate and soil conditions, it also characterizes each garden's style.

Good country living also means concern for environmental issues, featured these days on almost every news broadcast. As early as the 1970s, a farmers' cooperative near Le Mans linked quality free-range chicken production to the

The author's country garden on the edge of Provence blends Mediterranean essences such as olive trees with mountain woodland.

A bench beside the author's kitchen garden offers breaks from the toil of gardening, which is never finished but usually revitalizing in its own way.

replanting of ecologically balanced hedgerows torn up after the Second World War. Conservationist agencies established around the same time are now beginning to show results: the Conservatoire botanique de Brest, for example, one of the first in the world to specialize in saving threatened plants, now has its counterparts in each region, complemented by vast conservationist regional and national parks. Government organizations such as the Office national des forêts defend woodland, while the seafront agency, the Conservatoire du littoral, has worked so successfully that in 1999 French beaches were judged to be the cleanest in Europe. This agency also buys and restores historic gardens in a manner comparable to that of the National Trust in Britain, though only along France's coastlines. Meanwhile, city-dwellers are learning to discover, understand and protect their countryside thanks to recently created parks that include samples of local biotopes – Chalon and Limoges, for example.

Early efforts to protect rural landscapes imitated museum models that enclose still intact remnants. Today, the entire countryside is often regarded as a living landscape garden needing human care. After preservation comes enhancement. In 1999, the Green Meridian, a straight line of trees running from Dunkirk to Barcelona, was designed as part of a national millennium celebration. Landscape architects organizing the planting discovered much enthusiasm in small rural communities. Quality landscapes are everybody's business these days, for the many new 'grass-roots' associations as well as for big agencies. This very personal public involvement was immediately clear in the aftermath of the dreadful storms that battered France at the end of 1999.

Social structures have also been changing. Thirty years ago it was feared that rural regions, having lost their authentic peasant roots, could only be a comic-opera pastiche of the past revived for the superficial pleasure of passing tourists. Farmers were to be relegated to the demeaning role of caretakers. This has not happened. The French countryside is now far better maintained, with fewer ruins, better upkeep of roads and verges, new trails for hikers, bikers, horse-riders and walkers, and far less pollution than at any other time in recent history. And cultural life flourishes at the grass roots, too: there are more small publishing houses, village music schools, cybercafés and special-interest associations of all kinds than there have ever been. The very definitions of 'country' and 'city' are shifting: in 1998 it was estimated that half of the French countryside's inhabitants were of urban origin. Meanwhile, the garden renaissance affects cities as well: Paris alone has created 171 new gardens since 1980, many of which are designed to bring a bit of the countryside to the capital. City allotments now have long waiting lists. Small provincial communities ask for help from big-name gardening consultants. Aurillac, for example, a town of some 30,000 in the Massif Central, consulted the Design Workshop of the Conservatoire de Chaumont (*see page 164*) about creating new parks and gardens. The experts proposed integrating the town better into the beautiful local landscapes. In order to engage the interest of the town's park maintenance staff, they started off with a great Halloween festival in honour of Saint Pumpkin, an example of global influences being used for local causes. Local, national and global levels of communication connect more and more in deepest France, as you discover when the man who has been selling you cheese for twenty years at the village market enters the New York marathon.

Amateurs and professionals

Communications have also improved between amateur and professional gardeners. Indeed, it is sometimes hard to tell them apart. Home gardeners whose neighbours admire their creations may begin working for friends. Artists and sculptors turn to garden design as an original medium. Young enthusiasts have opened small specialist nurseries in remote regions, sometimes so successfully that many have been labelled collections of national interest. Above all, idealistic young people are discovering gardening as an absorbing and fulfilling vocation. I know personally of four instances where a young person has offered to help with an unusual garden, sacrificing financial security for the sake of participating in an ideal. This is symptomatic indeed: imaginative new gardens are often created by people under forty, starting with very few resources, who find in gardening not a leisure activity but a satisfying way of life.

The professional world has also evolved in recent years. In the wake of the 1968 student revolution, top French *paysagistes* (a term derived from '*paysage*', or 'landscape', and

The city of Blois has been innovative in its public garden designs, which include the Royal Gardens created by Gilles Clément opposite the château.

covering both landscape architects and designers) threw themselves into city-planning, social idealism and environmental projects. In 1974, the influential École d'horticulture de Versailles significantly renamed itself the École nationale supérieure du paysage. The school is where several of today's major figures first studied, and where some now teach. For decades, these mainly Parisian trendsetters dismissed home gardens as élitist, individualistic, nostalgic, incidental and *petit bourgeois*. Many, like Alain Roger, deplored the country-garden dream as sheer bucolic escapism. Some, such as Bernard Lassus, began exploring 'the spaces between', including motorway rest areas and industrial wastelands. The French version of the war between architects and plantsmen has always involved intellectual debate and political polemics. Not everyone takes sides, however: designer Alain Richert (*see page 80*) observed as recently as 1988 that country gardens often remained 'invertebrate' and unstructured, their owners assuming that plants alone could define a landscape. At the same time, the high buildings of city centres were surrounded by strongly defined architectural spaces with no plant interest whatsoever. Why, he pleaded, could we not imagine a new garden art blending the strengths of both Le Corbusier and William Robinson?

Things have changed. Parisian landscape architect Alexandre Chemetoff now connects the 'spaces between' to the restoration of geographical coherence – the continuity of valleys once cut up by motorways, for example. This pre-occupation with wholeness leads, he claims, directly back to the private garden, which has now become, in his view, a legitimate concern for professional designers. Lassus, his colleague, lately proclaimed that, 'The garden is the place for the inventions of our age.' Many designers like Richert take inspiration from the Brazilian Roberto Burle Marx, who combined harmoniously natural environments with formal design, plant-collecting and ecological awareness. At this level, too, there are young people discovering new vocations: the Paris garden-design studio of Brun and Péna, for instance, was founded by a former biochemist and an architect who became enthusiastic about landscape while on a walking tour of France.

Among these professionals, Gilles Clément stands out as an early defender of biological rather than architectural models, promoting dynamic and free-flowing styles (*see page 158*). Originator of the 'Planetary Garden' exhibit in Paris in 1999, he has become something of a guru in the gardening world. A novelist, plant-hunter and philosopher, as well as a designer of vast public projects, he refers to himself simply as a 'gardener'.

The new green tourism

Vigorous debates continue over the future of the French countryside. Participants as different as Augustin Berque (landscape philosopher), Jean Cabanel (of the Mission du Paysage) and Jacques Simon (land artist) agree that the hope for French agriculture lies in small-scale quality production, the development of personal craft industries, and 'green tourism'. Farmers struggling with bureaucracy in Brussels, with international trade pressures and with new computer equipment regularly rent vacation space to city folk, who in turn want quality products produced cleanly. Nothing illustrates current trends better than the creation all over France of outdoor 'ecomuseums' that are intended

to help preserve endangered rural traditions as well as flora and fauna, but also to propose models for a new rural economy. These sites invariably include gardens.

Garden-visiting is a major part of green tourism, and has taken the country by storm. Each spring weekend offers a wide choice between bountiful plant fairs and intellectual colloquiums on garden themes. More and more private gardens open regularly to the public all through the season, and regional brochures are available listing special visits for garden-heritage weekends in June and September.

But garden tourism in France must deal with government at all levels, for better or for worse. People struggling to restore or create gardens, or to establish plant fairs or garden associations, often complain that local authorities underestimate the economic potential of their efforts. Official tourist offices rarely know about local gardens, and even more rarely do they

Across France, ecomuseums such as this one in the Alsace have been set up to preserve country traditions, an important part of the new green tourism.

collaborate with the municipal parks department next door. An organization known as the Comité national pour le fleurissement de la France has done much to cut through the red tape, exerting great influence at the grass-roots level. Committee representatives scour the country making awards, not merely for pretty flower-boxes but also for such things as good town access, attractive traffic islands and effective landscape integration of water and roads – all concerns useful in promoting rural economies as well as local pride of place. Traffic roundabouts that flourish even in remote regions bear witness to the scope of gardening as a national passion. Some are created by departmental transport administrations, others by local municipalities. All are attempts at garden art, though kitsch is not always excluded. The Comité particularly recommends the roundabouts of Vannes in Brittany.

Art, gardens and garden art

At the Jardins de l'Albarède in the Dordogne, two young gardeners wondered what to do with a dead tree trunk. Ten years ago, they would have removed it as unsightly. Five years ago, they might have kept it as a habitat for wildlife. But they decided to streak it discreetly with dark-blue, grey and brown paint, transforming it into garden sculpture. Today, many other home gardeners regard their creations as art, too.

Everywhere in France is this convergence of the plastic arts and gardening apparent. French historians consider that 'landscape' is already a cultural and artistic concept, citing as an example the Romantic cult of mountain scenery, which was previously ignored or feared. Land art has been revived with a difference: an emphasis not on decay or sterile and inert materials but on the unpredictable ingredients of living materials and plant growth. As scholar John Dixon Hunt puts it, 'Land art seems to restore to landscape architecture its old and largely lost concern for the melding of site,

At the Jardins de l'Albarède in the Dordogne, a young couple with few resources other than imagination created sculpture from a dead tree trunk.

sight and insight.' And so in the new home gardens we have parsley rivers and lavender lakes. A good indicator of emerging trends is the French railway workers' gardening magazine, in which an editorialist judged in 1993 that, 'Today's gardener is not only a technician but also a philosopher and a poet, the person who makes, who creates.'

In the last ten years, I have made numerous prospecting trips thoughout the French provinces. I have found that today's French country gardens offer something for everyone, and not least for children. Their vitality offers one of the best hopes for the new millennium.

Louisa Jones
Ardèche, January 2000

INTIMATE COUNTRY GARDENS

Current fashion much admires a style that is sometimes called the '*jardin de curé*' (country priest's garden), sometimes the 'grandmother's garden', and sometimes both names together. Linked to childhood memories or to 'olden days', these gardens seem like fragments of a golden age, offering the comforts of 'mother earth' on the one hand, and of sacred ground on the other. Grandmothers and country priests, it is claimed, made do with basic resources, wasting nothing but creating gardens that nourished both body and spirit.

More and more French gardeners are inspired by this vision, which is at once very old and very new. Many find behind its high hedges or walls a refuge from modern stress. Inside, however, everything is exuberant vitality, an inter-mingling of flowers, vegetables, fruits and aromatics in an ever-shifting rainbow of soft fragrance and enticing nibbles. English writer Mirabel Osler, searching out the 'secret gardens' of France, describes this style as, 'the antithesis of everything I have been saying about the French predilec-tion for order … a way of arbitrary planting which has immediate charm: where peas, onions and forget-me-nots, growing in lackadaisical disarray, are divided by random grass and gravel paths, with a shadowy turbulence overhead from lilac, wisteria or apple trees. Somehow, in England you never come across this kind of planting.'

Le Jardin de la Pomme d'Ambre, created by Nicole Arboireau and her family, is highly individual but also typical of grandmothers' gardens today.

The style seems 'random' compared with classical canons: its design is not logically linked to house architecture, not even as an outdoor room. It is a world apart – though not far off – always enclosed. All sense of scale disappears in spaces that become impossible to read logically, hence full of adventure. Are formal geometries allowed? Opinions differ: the traditional idea of the *jardin de curé* would suggest box-edged paths in cross shapes around a central fountain, but current practice favours dabs over lines, echoes of Impressionist luxuriance. Any constructions must be only partly visible, soft toned, picturesque and ageing – paint is always peeling. Climbers and ramblers run through hedges and half cover roofs. The gardener values chance offerings, either from neighbours or from heaven itself: self-sown poppies may smother vegetables, while

Luxuriant vegetation in gardens such as the Bayols' may half smother objects that are unique, personal, creative and even eccentric, but always welcoming.

marigolds protect them. Riotous colour may also seem haphazard, not carefully modulated. Dahlias, sunflowers, love-lies-bleeding and cannas are not considered too vulgar for this fashion, which appreciates annuals and biennials. In this personal paradise, work becomes pleasure, and harmony with nature prevails. The gardener welcomes wildlife and is philosophical about pests, trying 'soft' controls and gentle guidance when possible. Ponds shelter fish, dragonflies, amphibians. This is an Eden where the snake is invited to stay for dinner. The cat is also almost always present … perhaps because it is sensual, domestic and wild all at once, as well as being a good companion for intimate gardening.

Research suggests that real French priests' gardens were and are quite different from this idyllic vision. But today's intimate country style is Romantic, drawing its energy from dream rather than from historical veracity. In this it is comparable with other contemporary Romantic gardening styles, such as the Dutch fashion for creating islands of wilderness in one of the world's most artificial landscapes. As usual in Romanticism, a good deal of art goes into the illusion of spontaneity. Thus, it is no surprise that the *jardin de curé*, with its emphasis on personal creativity, is the genre most beloved by writers and artists. Its roots feed more on the novel than on Church history – on Rousseau, Bernardin de Saint-Pierre, Balzac, George Sand, Proust and Colette; perhaps also on sentimental folk art and the idealizing of Impressionist painters: Monet's garden at Giverny might be considered one of its most compelling models.

Writers and film-makers particularly cherish this style. In 1979 Pierre Gascar entitled a pioneer book *Le Jardin de curé*, in which he described his secret world tucked into a corner of a medieval abbey in the Jura. A picturesque peasant garden is still visible today just inside these walls.

Gascar's refuge has not lain entirely undiscovered, however: Jean Marais picked salads there for the film adaptation of Victor Hugo's *Les Misérables*. Another example of this fashion is Claude Pigeard's garden near Paris. Formerly a Renault factory worker, Pigeard quit his job in 1968 to restore his childhood home, a picturesque village curate's residence, which he has surrounded with a lush garden. Bertrand Tavernier shot scenes here for his film *A Day in the Country*, which is full of Impressionist echoes.

Real country grandmothers today are often suburban. Nicole Arboireau, in her book *Les Jardins de grand-mère*, describes several ladies gardening unselfconsciously among colourful jumbles of flowers, vegetables and odd objects. Husbands can sometimes impose order – straight rows and cut edges – where the women indulge in spontaneous over-spilling. These grandmothers' realms are the domestic equivalent of working-class allotments, where traditionally women were not allowed. They are not at all nostalgic and just a bit 'tasteless' for the fashionable vision of city-dwellers and the gardening press. Great designers may now admire plaster dwarfs, but the middle-class home gardener hesitates still.

Other grandmothers, equally unselfconscious, produce results more in keeping with current fashion. In Normandy, a doctor's wife decided not to be a painter like her mother. Instead, she created a wonderful walled garden where colour surges like waves. An expert delphinium breeder, she had a nursery until her husband's retirement. At the Château de Mongenan near Bordeaux, a mother-and-daughter team of vintners cultivates a luxuriant sunken garden said to have been designed by Rousseau himself. Florence Mothe, the daughter, has also become a successful food and garden writer.

Today's intimate country style has deep roots in French family life. Certainly the trend is nostalgic, echoing memo-

Designer Camille Muller took inspiration from his grandmother's Alsatian garden for his Paris rooftop, even including the gnomes.

ries of childhood, and seeking to preserve old lore, skills and heirloom plant varieties. But this dream is also strongly linked to individual self-expression, to imagination, to art. In both respects, it offers a viable future model for home gardeners of all ages. With the start of a new millennium, everyone wants the 'old-fashioned' country garden's vital exuberance, its economy and common sense, its celebration of life in small spaces, its sensuous satisfactions, its harmony with the natural world and its scope for creative invention.

NICOLE ARBOIREAU

A Grandmother on the Riviera

Nicole Arboireau came to the French Riviera as a child of seven when her father was employed as a railway station agent at Fréjus. Her family lived in an abandoned belle époque villa, its garden dense with orange groves, rambling roses, jasmine and whispering eucalyptus. For some forty years after that idyllic initiation, she has watched the region change drastically. She now lives in a 1960s suburb of Fréjus, built along the Via Aurélia, an ancient Roman road. Here, she has created a magical garden with the help of her husband, son, daughter and now grandchildren. She thinks about both her soil's heritage and her grandchildren's future.

Along this stretch of the Côte d'Azur are some of Europe's grandest gardens, intimidating sometimes for gardeners of modest means. But on Nicole's two thousand square metres, imagination and energy compensate for everything. The plot is disadvantaged in several respects: almost completely encircled by neighbours, it can be reached only by a narrow drive past another house. Then, it is very steeply graded and contains large, voracious trees – cork oaks, a magnificent pepper

The playhouse built by Nicole Arboireau's family for her granddaughter has two 'dragons' (*Beschorneria yuccoïodes*) guarding its entrance.

tree, Aleppo pines and three eucalyptus. Nicole's husband helped by transforming the slope into a labyrinth of narrow curving terraces, using stone for walls and, for steps, bits of railway sleepers allowed to weather to the same grey as the stone. As you circle round, you often have your nose and eyes at the level above, so that these 'drawers' become display cases for Nicole's many treasures. Terracing further allows sun-loving plants to receive the sun, even through the trees. The latter's lower branches are clipped to admit light and air, and their trunks make frames and curtains which help preserve the individual character of each corner. Nicole refuses to be daunted by the reputation of pines and eucalyptus. It is true that in this crowded garden some shrubs are less dense in habit and not so rampant as elsewhere, but this, she claims, allows for more layering. Tree trunks are also used to support climbers – tough ones. In one case, the coils of a wisteria are already encircling the tall straight bole of an Aleppo pine and beginning to squeeze. Will the pine be able to adjust, perhaps growing around the wisteria and incorporating it? Nicole watches with interest and without anxiety. Gardens are full of combat situations, she says, it's up to them to fight it out.

21

When Nicole and her husband first arrived here some fifteen years ago, most of their neighbours were clearing out all existing vegetation and putting up hedges of the ubiquitous Arizona blue cypress. Nicole insisted on waiting to see 'what the birds sowed' before planting. These included wild oleanders along the stream, now rare in the area. Nicole has also saved many plants from bulldozers in other housing developments, such as a spiny acacia from a park in nearby Cavalière. She likes its leathery lavender-brown seed pods almost as much as its furry, sulphur-yellow balls. In spite of being allergic to them, she grows some thirteen varieties of winter-flowering acacia. She loves yellow, and is moving towards brighter and brighter colours, including a 'Brazilian' terrace where fuchsia and orange tones congregate audaciously. She admires the rambling rose 'Albéric Barbier', with its fresh butter-coloured blossoms and scent like unripe apples. No matter if iridescent rose beetles love it, too – there is enough for everyone.

Most of her plants have a story. Her white camellias were first grown by a retired Middle Eastern tea-planter. Ill health forced him to abandon some three hundred potted cuttings, and the nursery man who took them on offered many to Nicole and her garden club. There is a large planting of scilla bulbs, which she says are mistakenly called 'Peruvian'. Grown in all Riviera gardens, these were once made into omelettes used to poison rats. She admires a large shrub rose, *Rosa Indica major*, the botanic variety used by the perfume industry in Grasse for centuries. She has placed it between a pale-blossomed lilac bush and a feathery tamarisk. Or the rambling 'American Pillar', introduced with great success to the Riviera in the 1930s, when it was planted around many railway stations. Nicole has been asked to lecture on local plant lore at the horticultural school in Grasse.

She cherishes the common cottage plants: hellebores, kerria, beauty bush, spiraeas, Japanese quince. But she has also garden varieties of local wild plants – many cistus, some acanthus – and common Riviera exotics: steel-blue echium spires and yellow-blossomed euryops. In autumn, the many perennial sages take the stage, along with bright-yellow cassias. Visual unity is provided by the steel-blue paint of all the wooden structures – pergolas, tables, low fences. This dazzling colour was produced by the haphazard mixing of paint bought in a sale.

Pergolas and other wooden supports in the garden provide more planting space, as well as shade where needed – here with *Rosa laevigata*.

There are many thorny and even poisonous plants in this garden, including a collection of solanums in pots at the turn of a path. Nicole's seven-year-old granddaughter listens carefully when told that mahonia fruit are 'blueberries meant only for the birds'. She knows that her grandmother is something of a witch, and aspires to become a sorcerer's apprentice. The whole family built her playhouse, and now two giant biscorneria are like dragons guarding her secret cave. The little girl also wanted nearby a giant fennel (*Ferula communis*), which, soft in texture but sinewy, was once used to whip children – 'This way she can keep her eye on it', says Nicole wryly.

The writer Colette romanticized her mother's garden, claiming that within its walls, for thirty years, no children fought, no voice was raised, and all neighbours lived in harmony. Nicole has no patience with such sentimentality. On her upper west corner lives a man of strict order who is interested only in vegetables. When Nicole's Mermaid rose wanders over at will, she tells the neighbour to cut off whatever bothers him. When his Niçois squash vine winkles its way through the hedge and begins to produce fruit on her side, he cuts that off, too. She considers him quite a character, and no doubt he returns the compliment.

Nicole herself grows few edibles, much to her mother's regret, only salads, herbs and some fruit, such as the persimmons she likes to fill with rum and eat with a spoon in the autumn. But few gardens are more sensuous than this one. Having noticed that many local grandmothers' gardens contain shrines to the Virgin Mary, she decided to include one in her own garden – but dedicated to Bacchus, in honour of a family friend who regularly worships the *vin rosé* of the region. But were Madonna lilies then appropriate? Always one to dig into old gardening books, Nicole

Nicole Arboireau's house nearly disappears under rambling plants. Ceanothus thrives at her doorstep, loving the Riviera climate.

found a Renaissance description of this plant which attributes it to Venus because of its 'shameful pistils'. She is leaving it there.

Everything here is richly invested with imagination, memory and creativity. Advising beginners, Nicole refuses to give recipes and strict rules. Study the past, she recommends, but stay open to the unforeseen that life will inevitably provide. Let the plants do what they like best, and, above all, make a garden that looks like yourself.

A profusion of pots

The problem of rooty soil is partly solved by pots, which abound in all sizes and situations: flanking the top of the stairs, grouped on or around painted metal tables, or half buried at the base of big trees. Pots also provide more planting space for the broken shoots, pruned rose clippings and self-sown plantlets that Nicole recycles in a huge cauldron full of compost. She also makes new pots from old shards, mending them with big iron staples that will rust becomingly, and lining them with cement. The patchwork effect only adds to their charm.

A Painter's Family Garden in Provence

Doudou Bayol's family have been market gardeners in Saint-Rémy-de-Provence for generations. But one forebear, Joseph Roumanille, became a great Provençal poet whose first collection of verse was called *Daisies*. Roumanille's father sold produce, however, and his epitaph read: 'A Gardener and a Good and Estimable Man'. Doudou is certainly his worthy descendant. She in turn married another Joseph, a painter who regularly chooses her garden as a favourite subject.

This family and this town have made amazing leaps from its provincial past into the global age. In the nineteenth century, Saint-Rémy was known as 'Garden City' for its intensive vegetable production. Today, it is a jet-set rendezvous, attracting fashion magnates and royalty alike. Doudou grew up in her parents' eighteenth-century farmstead. Some thirty years ago, she and Joseph built a new house across the road, and now their daughter Jeanne is fixing up the old family home. With her husband, Jeanne restores and sumptuously furnishes old gypsy caravans, selling them to top Parisian decorators, who may then ship them to America. Doudou's garden has been discovered by internationally

known garden photographers in search of 'authentic' rustic refinement. The Bayols have successfully combined peasant roots with cosmopolitan elegance, not only because today's sophisticates want what this family has had for centuries, but also because of the kind of people they are.

When Doudou began to garden here in the 1970s, she welcomed newcomers who opened up fresh horizons for her. Today, she travels to North Africa to buy jewelry and pottery for the Bayols' garden gallery. It is all hard work: she sets up and hangs all the shows on her own. She also helps look after six grandchildren and tends the garden alone. Every twelve months for years she has cleaned out the irrigation canals (*roubines*) that edge her land, spreading the mud around to enrich the garden. 'Use what you already have at hand,' she says proudly, 'that's the peasant tradition.' Despite the hard work, she finds gardening restorative: 'It is my best medicine,' she says, 'I tried yoga, but nothing makes me feel as good as gardening.'

Her thousand-square-metre plot, with its vestigial cherry orchard, is enclosed to the north by the gallery and the house, which is visible behind cascades of wisteria on the broad trellising only as glimpses of teal-blue shutter. All other sides are planted with those tall cypress hedges which

The Bayol garden can seem like a miniature jungle right next to the house, but the basket for picking cherries is never far away.

outline market-gardening plots all over the area. Doudou's poet-ancestor Roumanille once described dining with his parents 'in the mottled shade of a grape arbour', just as Doudou's family does today. She likes the gradual unfolding of her space from the almost-smothered patios by the house to the sunnier, wilder spaces at the far end.

Soil is only fifty centimetres deep, so that the roots of several old cherry trees run horizontally under garden plantings on top of a layer of clay. In spite of these drawbacks, the garden's dense plantings thrive under Doudou's watchful care. In early years, she simply sowed a package of mixed annuals known in France as '*gazon japonais*'. Then she began to fill this in with plants given by friends – she still loves to say, for example, 'That's Jean-Marie's oleander!' Two little palm trees that she found self-sown in a workman's yard are now solid presences by the pond. Which variety? 'The hardy kind', she says, and so they have proven to be. She abandoned fragile plants long ago, and keeps nothing that cannot take an occasional ten or twelve degrees below zero in winter. But this kind of gardening has so many sheltered spaces that she is able to keep an orange abutilon outdoors all year round. She loves the old cottage plants, carefully replacing a dead weigela, but she also adores white fuchsias, and has a collection of rare hortensias … in pots.

Water is not a problem here, with a stream running through the heart of the garden and the agricultural com-

munity's irrigation canals on all sides. Doudou also dug the pond herself – 'I wanted something larger but that was all we could afford.' This is a garden which she considers has grown slowly, step by step. At the same time, it is constantly changing. Her columbines were crowded out by Japanese impatience that she introduced with hedgerow seed, and they have now emigrated to the north side of the house. Always twice the size of any others in the neighbourhood, they grow thick once more. 'One good thing about being a grandmother', says Doudou, 'is that I now appreciate all the seasons', from the first snowdrop to the 'yellow autumn crocuses' (*Sternbergia lutea*), which still take her by surprise, year after year. 'When I was young I wanted fine weather all the time,' she notes, 'but now I need the changing seasons.'

Doudou also feels right at home with organic methods, which she has always practised, never spraying except for hosing off blackfly, or putting Bordeaux mixture (copper sulphate) on the fruit trees. That special colour of faded turquoise has become one of the French countryside's most characteristic hues.

The Bayol's old cat now sleeps its life away under the southern trellis. A new addition west of the house, with another veranda, sports a feeder that is hotly disputed by both birds and red squirrels, and Doudou could spend hours watching them if she had the time. But she also cooks a lot, preparing all the food served at gallery openings herself, canning peaches and making *fromage de tête* (pork brawn). Her own garden is full of herbs and fruit, but with a family of market gardeners, she does not grow her own vegetables. In a year or so, her daughter Jeanne will help run the gallery, and Doudou will have more time to garden.

Fields near the house once used for market gardening are now ploughed yearly to attract these vibrant poppies.

Doudou Bayol's poet-ancestor Roumanille enjoyed eating in the 'mottled shade of a grape arbour'. Today, wisteria serves the purpose.

Will Saint-Rémy be spoiled by the influx of city sophisticates? As long as there is an active peasant population, Doudou judges, there can be mutual enrichment and common benefits. When the farmers disappear, the towns die … and the intimate country dream turns into dead décor. But if everyone evolves as well as the Bayols have done, there is hope for the future. Meanwhile, their garden seems timeless. Vincent van Gogh admired not far away the 'farm gardens, with their lovely big red Provençal roses, and the vines and the fig trees! It is all a poem!' He might have been describing Doudou Bayol's garden in Saint-Rémy-de-Provence.

Work and pleasure

Work, leisure, pleasure – these terms change meanings in such a garden, where deck-chairs beckon in tall grass, and Joseph picks cherries for breakfast from overhead boughs. As in his paintings, the floral luxuriance always offers a welcoming point of entry, a place to rest. Old objects anchor lush greenery, both in Doudou's garden and in Joseph's pictures – tasteful here, nothing junky, but always worn with real use. Time and effort provide a mellow ripening as nothing else can.

Amazing colour

Van Gogh celebrated the 'amazing colour' of the 'small peasant garden' he painted in 1889. The Bayols' garden and some of Joseph's paintings echo Impressionist scenes from Argenteuil or Giverny, whose bright dabs, according to historian Michel Baridon, owed much to the recent importation of exotic flowers and the development of industrial dyes. Today, in Doudou's painterly garden, splashes of bright colour continue to blur any lines or plan throughout the season. There are even stunning wild-flower meadows – Doudou encourages wild poppies in spring by fresh ploughing. In this, once more, old country ways rejoin current cosmopolitan fashion.

A Parisian Designer's Rooftop Garden

Camille Muller is the preferred garden designer of fashion sophisticates and avant-garde artists. He is famous for his technical feats in Parisian courtyards and his 'wild' style in larger spaces. In his forties, sporting black leather and never quite clean shaven, he might be the adventuresome Rimbaud of the garden world. But if he offers the poet's 'incredible Floridas' to his clients, he saves the 'panther eyes and rainbows' for home – a Parisian rooftop. His inspiration remains deeply rooted in his Alsatian childhood and his grandmother's country garden.

Literally rooted, in fact. Just ten years ago, Camille helped his grandmother weed her vegetables in Alsace, then packed up all the rejects: brambles, a wild rose and some euonymus, which he planted in her honour in one box on his roof. The rose always blooms for Mother's Day, he says proudly.

Camille is perhaps more sentimental than his grandmother would be, but everything he creates is based literally on solid foundations. Technology and poetry are his twin goals. He takes as a model the fine craftsmen who for centuries made furniture in the Saint-Antoine neighbourhood of Paris where he has chosen to live. He found his

On just a hundred square metres of rooftop, Camille Muller grows *Vitis coignetiae*, *Clematis montana*, *Akebia quinata* and even a Mermaid rose.

house by chance when, homesick for the country, he walked down a narrow hallway to emerge in a tiny open courtyard where chimney swifts wheeled in the sunlight. Here was a patch of 'nourishing soil' in contrast with the city paving. The buildings were an unreadable shambles, which he acquired piecemeal and restored, little by little, with his own hands. Camille's father came from home to inspect, took one look, and advised him to sell again immediately. But Muller remains captivated by this tiny bit of country life in the heart of the city's bustle where the courtyard (twenty-five square metres) has been extended by roughly a hundred square metres of roof garden. It remains a refuge garden – but not for resting. Muller experiences it is a kind of playground, a testing place for new ideas, a dynamic, ever-changing space with a mood of adventure.

Structures up on the roof needed careful planning. Camille installed a strong steel cross-beam which now supports his wooden-plank terrace and the heaviest containers. None of the planters are set directly on the roof but stand on ledges or are hung with hooks from the walls. Their supports are coated not with zinc but with lead, which can be walked on. Boardwalks and painted metal steps allow access to all parts and levels. Neighbouring buildings and

The entrance courtyard, only twenty-five square metres, is a miniature well of sunshine enclosed by Virginia creeper and black-stemmed bamboo.

tree-tops from nearby streets almost entirely enclose this roof, however, providing wind protection. The highest point of the garden can be reached precariously by climbing a ladder up a neighbouring wall to a suspended metal platform. From here you can look directly down onto the whole garden as into a well. Only recently did Muller install some simple guard-rails by the lower steps – round lengths of grey-painted iron that melt unobtrusively into the whole. The effect is like a ship's rigging – a pirate's stronghold, says

Muller – or a tree house. Delighted visitors make comparisons with their grandmothers' gardens, or with houses in Bali or California. Lanterns light up the garden at night.

The interior of the building remains a complex of seemingly haphazard spaces with multiple perspectives, many levels and crossing points of view. The upper-level windows let in light from all directions, while creating a sort of loggia effect around the roof. Thus, garden and house thread together in a play of light and shade shifting from hour to hour, and from season to season.

Muller has training both as a plantsman and as a designer, first with Marie Mallet at the Bois des Moutiers gardens in Normandy, then with Gilles de Brissac at Apremont, and finally with Gilles Clément, famous for his 'wild' gardens (*see page 158*). At home, Muller's small jungle intermingles cottage plants with exotics. Chance determines many choices: roses left over from a garden show, items that clients have rejected, sick specimens no one could cure, and his grandmother's weeds … all risks he can allow himself only at home. In the courtyard, bamboos dominate: *Semi-arundinaria fastuosa* soars to eleven metres high, flanked by *Phyllostachys nigra*. These are set off by delicate *Aralia elata* and pots of shade-tolerant impatience around a tiny fountain. On the north wall grow three intermingled masses of common ivy and Virginia creeper, as well as *Vitis coignetiae*, all pruned hard on ground level but allowed to explode up there in the light. These climbers, he feels, symbolically link earth and sky while providing seasonal variations of colour and texture. The number of birds nesting in their foliage and in the bamboo can make such a clamour on summer evenings that conversation becomes impossible. Pruning, however, requires a giant ladder, a sense of adventure and a talent for acrobatics.

Clematis montana, *Akebia quinata*, morning glory, periwinkle and even a Mermaid rose also grow on the upper level. Containers support shrubs and small trees such as *Sorbaria sorbifolia* or a spray of giant *Miscanthus*. City microclimates being warmer, Muller can even manage Mexican orange (*Choisya ternata*) in a sheltered corner. In city gardens, moreover, he recommends planting shade-lovers in half shade, and giving full sun to those grown elsewhere in half shade.

Upkeep consists mainly of ensuring that downspouts and the drip irrigation system remain clear. Because part of the run-off goes into the pool below, plants are fed with only natural substances – dried blood and bone meal once a year – so as not to poison the fish. For the same reason, his plants here are never sprayed with chemicals. There are slugs and snails, but the many birds in the garden keep them under control. Muller has noticed that his sparrows even eat blackfly. This world has, he feels, its own coherence, its own balance of natural processes. He intervenes, of course, but takes his cue from what occurs spontaneously.

He loves all the garden's inhabitants. Here, too, the local and the exotic coexist in harmony. Bats, butterflies, swifts, sparrows and blackbirds find refuge in Muller's climbers, out of reach of the elegant cat Nocibé, named after her birthplace in Madagascar. A tiny Oriental wooden house by the hearth shelters a family of crickets – the kind that in northern France survive near bakers' ovens and now can be found in the warmth of the Paris metro system. In Muller's house they roam freely, and their chirping often competes successfully with the birdsong.

The objects, he says, are there to make you dream – a clothes-line with multicoloured plastic pegs echoes Rimbaud's 'rainbows stretched like bridles'. And everywhere, peeking through the ivy, are Muller's famous dwarfs.

They mean many things to him: nostalgia again for his Alsatian childhood, a very avant-garde appreciation of humour in gardens, rebellion against conventional canons of taste. But, he admits ruefully, 'It's even worse than that. I find them heart-warming.'

Kitsch or art? Whichever it may be, Muller has united all the conventions of the new French country garden: intimacy, spontaneity and luxuriance in a composition where the house does not dominate; an intermingling of fruit, herbs, flowers and vegetables with found objects; spaces for living, not merely looking, where fauna feels welcome. Above all, this is a garden of deeply personal creativity where the past once again nourishes the future.

Careful construction was necessary to support the weight of planter boxes and pots, so that climbing aloft is magical but not dangerous.

The country in the city

On excursions outside town, Muller picks roadside flowers for bouquets, which at home he sets on the courtyard table. His rooftop planters overspill with brick-red pelargoniums intermingling with wallflowers, lobelia, nasturtiums and Herb Robert, the latter cheerfully self-sowing. He also grows there a dwarf apple tree, raspberry canes, a grapevine, many salad greens and herbs, a robust kale, even a pumpkin vine. Every year he adds a few tomato plants supplied by his parents' potager in Alsace. His efficient downspouts were inspired by farmers' rain barrels. And of course his dwarfs all have country cousins …

2

A PASSION
FOR PLANTS

In the beginning was botany. Many French cities today still have active botanical gardens that were first founded by medieval medical faculties. Then came the globe-scouting plant-finders. Contemporary designer Bernard Lassus has baptized his park surrounding the marine citadel at Rochefort 'Homecoming Gardens' ('Jardins des retours'), in honour of men such as the monk Charles Plumier, who in 1690 brought back from South America six little plants to which the then intendant at Rochefort, Michel Bégon, gave his name. There were also humbler versions of the roving plant-collectors: Breton writer Châteaubriand observed in 1788 the gardens of 'every peasant, sailor or labourer', where 'among the pot herbs, gooseberries, roses, iris, and pot marigolds could be found a tea plant from Cayenne, tobacco from Virginia, a flower from China, some echo of another coast and another sun'.

Many fine plant collections were destroyed during the Second World War, both on the north-western coasts and along the French Riviera. But courageous enthusiasts soon began again: the Mallet family, for instance, restored their 1898 Lutyens-Jekyll property in Varengeville, Normandy, while their neighbour Princess Sturdza began work on Le Vastérival. Similarly, the La Rochefoucauld family planted the Arboretum des Grandes Bruyères near Orléans and began the Parcs et jardins de France to subsidize historic

Euphorbia characias at the Bellevue gardens of Martine Lemonnier may not be rare but it is still beautiful.

French collectors today enjoy their treasures as an integrated part of a pleasing garden scene, as here at the Château de Momas near Pau.

In 1973, these collectors, and others like Jacques Gérard, whose family has owned the Arboretum de la Fosse north of Tours since 1751, founded the prestigious Association des parcs botaniques de France (APBF). It first obtained government protection of important collections, then went on to inventory the woody plants of France. In 1990 it set up a collectors' network, the Conservatoire de collections végétales spécialisées (CCVS), working closely with the long-established Société nationale d'horticulture de France. Today, the CCVS has its own journal, *Hommes et plantes*, and confers 'National Collection' labels all over the hexagon. The little-known city of Melle in the Poitou region, for example, boasts official labels for *Aesculus*, *Betula*, *Fraxinus*, *Salix*, *Sorbus* and *Tilia* along a remarkable 'Discovery Walk'. Many such titles are held today by young owners of serious specialist nurseries.

Patrice and Hélène Fustier first organized a plant exchange at their Château de Courson near Paris for members of the APBF in 1982. This has now evolved into a great biannual event which draws visitors from all over the world. English garden photographer Roger Phillips wrote about it in 1990: 'The flower show was terrific. There is a whole new generation of French plantsmen: young, vital, keen and most of them specialising in one area of rarities or another ...'. The show continues to thrive. Less well known outside France are the small plant fairs in every market town, and the growing numbers of small family nurseries, often just barely managing on a shoestring, which supply them.

The major change of recent years has indeed been the spread of this passion from an élite to people of more modest means and all backgrounds. Home gardeners of every sort have become collectors. South of Paris at Lardy, Anne-Marie and her husband Yonn raised three children while devoting every spare moment to a garden of only

restorations. The Vicomte de Noailles planted his olive-bearing terraces on the Riviera, while organizing garden excursions for likeminded owners. During one of these trips, Prince Wolkonsky, creator of Kerdalo in Brittany, discovered Dr Favier's reviving gardens near Cherbourg. Friends remember their eternal debate: were they collecting for botanical interest or for aesthetics, for botany or for horticulture? English connections were crucial in those formative years – Harold Hillier, Roy Lancaster and Lionel Fortescue contributed a great deal.

1,100 square metres, the beauty of which has drawn photographers from all over the world; its collections are rich enough to merit inclusion in the *Guide des jardins botaniques de France*. Little-known regions like the Aquitaine are producing a remarkable range of family gardens as well as impressive nursery collections: the Plantarium at Gaujacq, Côté Sud des Landes, the bamboos of Planbuisson and Michel Lumen's wetland plants are among them. At La Sedelle in the Limousin, also a developing region, Philippe Wanty created a maple-and-prunus arboretum in a 'natural' valley garden. On a single day he may receive both a busload of curious *gendarmes* and their families and a journalist from *Vogue*. All over the country, creativity goes hand in hand with connoisseurship. No one wants to choose between botany and horticulture, everyone wants both.

These examples also illustrate a trend towards organizing even tiny gardens into a sequence of different biotopes, each suited to a particular group of plants. Les Jardins d'Agapanthe in upper Normandy, created in 1995 by a young designer and his mother, display an amazing itinerary through an area of just 5,000 square metres: a Sequoia avenue, a 'kalapanax terrace', a wild nook, collections of agapanthus, veronica, sedum and daphne, a 'euphorbia amphitheatre', an 'English border', an exotic garden, a sunken garden, a series of ponds, a small outdoor theatre and a tearoom.

West of Orléans, Pierre Paris, working with nothing but his gardener's salary from the Parc floral de la Source, planted a remarkable, hauntingly beautiful *Ilex* collection on marshy land near the Loire. It is open only one morning a week so as not to disturb his experiments. 'Why do people collect plants?' he asks, suggesting an answer: 'passion, tenacity, friendship and human warmth, complicity' and the pleasures of 'learning to share and appreciate the differences between species'. He adds: 'Creating a collection is a long, difficult task which may take a lifetime; but this quest, for me, is a source of harmony.'

Today, this country of four hundred cheeses is enjoying biodiversity as a new kind of connoisseurship. Global plant-collecting continues, but with care to avoid invasive imports. In the following examples, three very different collectors indulge their passion for its own sake, but also practise the art of gardening as a whole.

At the La Verderonne gardens in Picardy, Dr Henri Cassoly displays extensive collections of clematis and old roses in many different settings.

Gentle Exoticism in the Heart of Normandy

Martine and François Lemonnier opened their nursery north of Rouen in 1983. They were soon familiar figures at plant fairs all over the region and quickly obtained the CCVS (National Collection) label for meconopsis and hellebores. Only in 1994 did they officially open their display garden, Bellevue, where you can take a trip around the world without losing sight of the rolling hills, pastureland and beech forests of upper Normandy.

The story, now legendary, is that in 1981 François was a country doctor, and Martine busy with drawing and tapestry, when they took a holiday and happened upon a carpet of blue Welsh poppy in bloom at Savill Gardens. Inspired and unable to find *Meconopsis betonicifolia* for sale, Martine managed the very difficult task of growing some from seed. The Botanical Gardens of Edinburgh graciously offered her more seed for other meconopsis, and the collection began to build. The nursery started almost by itself. Today, the thatched cottage of François's family property at Bellevue houses offices and three bed-and-breakfast rooms. The couple's daughter Lucie and her husband Patrice are taking over the business so that the older genera-

At the Jardins de Bellevue, rare species settle into surroundings that produce a feeling of harmony and well-being in the beholder, connoisseur or not.

tion can devote all of its time to plant reproduction and the creation of ever new gardens on the six hectares of surrounding land. One of François's brothers has become the family plant-hunter, making expeditions all over the globe.

In the two categories for which they have labelled collections, the Lemonniers especially like, among the meconopsis, *Meconopsis punicea*, *M. superba*, *M. dhwojii*, *M. quintuplinervia*, *M. horridula alba*, *M.* x *sheldonii* 'Branklyn' and many cultivars of *M. napaulensis*; and among the hellebores, beautiful cultivars of *Helleborus niger*, *H.* x *orientalis* and *H.* x *ericsmithii* syn. x *nigercors*. Besides these specialities, the gardens at Bellevue now display an impressive range of snowdrops, primroses, tropaeolum, hardy geraniums, foxgloves, tree peonies, hydrangeas and greenhouse treasures, along with an extensive arboretum. None of the plantings appear regimented; all have settled into surroundings that not only make them happy but produce a feeling of harmony and well-being in the beholder.

Martine has always loved reading about the great plant expeditions. She wanted to know where her treasures came from and how they arrived. 'This is very much a travel garden', she says with pride. She admires the missionary George Forrest, who brought home 100,000 cuttings. 'I don't know if he converted many Chinese,' she comments, 'but he certainly was a great collector!' The Abbé Delayey's Himalayan plants are well represented, not only by the meconopsis but also by rhododendrons and the fir *Abies delavayi*. 'Of course, you can walk around here without knowing the stories of the plants,' says François, 'but you miss a lot.' He likes the tale of the *Prunus mume* 'Taï Aku', much loved by the Japanese but lost entirely after a blight. Known only in old prints, it was miraculously rediscovered in a private garden near London, and has now been reintroduced into Japan.

In this garden, concentrations of floral colour are always surrounded by high hedges, so that the trees and larger shrubs blend without brightness into the green landscape beyond. 'Green is restful,' explains Martine, 'and colour disturbs. This is a place of peace, of reflection in tranquillity.' One of the newer enclosed plantings is a contrast garden with red and black on one side facing silver and white on the other. This spot was once a farmer's dumping place, later invaded by tough wild willows. It took five years to prepare it for planting, including bringing in truckloads of earth to raise the outer edge. Then, when Martine found herself with two parallel sixty-metre-long borders, she nearly lost courage. She bought black plastic at the local farmers' cooperative and set out her plants in holes. They grew twice as fast as elsewhere. Now she adds: 'I've removed more plants here than I left', citing a peony that turned out to be too orange a tone when next to a darker red.

Even in the brighter floral displays, colours remain ever soft and soothing. The former kitchen garden is another secret space, as is the peony garden or the hydrangea border, where a stand of *Hydrangea paniculata* is set off by an elegant raspberry-and-pearl chrysanthemum named 'Empéreur de Chine'.

Elsewhere, bloom serves to light up shady undergrowth: it is in the Himalayan border, where the meconopsis are surrounded by plants from their home region to extend the

planting's flowering season. These include collections of primroses and ferns, of members of the *Araceae* family such as arisaemas, of bulbs like the Himalayan *Cardiocrinum giganteum* var. *yunnanense*, and of Nepal lilies. In summer and autumn, the soft tones of *Hydrangea aspera* 'Macrophylla' subsp. *sargentiana* and those of the *Villosa* group provide floral and foliage variety. Martine especially cherishes her Chinese peonies, which flower at the same time as the poppies: the *emodi* species has large, white, very pure flowers, its buds opening over a long period of time. There are even dwarf tree peonies like the pale-yellow-flowering *Paeonia veitchii*, which is only thirty centimetres high.

Just as each space has its surprises, so does each season. Spring starts early when the hellebores overlap with magnolias, followed by flowering cherries, dogwoods and other spring shrubs. May, when gardens everywhere else are bursting with brilliance, is a low point at Bellevue – at least insofar as flowers are the main point of the garden. François loves the fresh green of new foliage at this time. Some plants, like the easy-to-grow *Tilia henryana*, have copper-coloured new growth. Soon the meconopsis begin their display, followed by the hydrangeas. Always, the Lemonniers opt for subtlety.

Expansion never stops. A lower pasture with two big ponds will turn into a wild-flower meadow. Room will be found for brother Alexis's growing collection of old Norman roses. Research into nineteenth-century rose-growers around Rouen has led him as far as Australia to recuperate cuttings, which then need to be checked against sources and old descriptions to determine authenticity. 'You have to be patient', says Martine with a sigh.

The Jardins de Bellevue hold National Collection labels (CCVS) for both meconopsis and hellebores, including *Helleborus orientalis* 'Black Cup'.

The Jardins de Bellevue blend into the surrounding countryside through a careful use of scale and mood in all seasons.

Visitors are sometimes disappointed by the lack of brilliant show, but this garden's delicacy, the extreme richness of its collections and the knowledge of its creators, both botanical and historical, are its strongest points. Whatever takes shape in the future will surely maintain the harmonious proportions, the soft lines and tones, the generous volumes of the existing park. This will remain a discovery garden, a trip around the world, but one in which visitors always feel at home.

Autumn and winter

Autumn colour at Bellevue is particularly magnificent. The parrotia turn to flame as early as August. But the best autumn season is November, when the maples, beech and oak are all at their peak, as are the shrubby dogwoods, hydrangeas, euonymus, viburnums and cotinus. The liquidambar cultivars alone offer every shade from pale blond to deep carmine. Martine wonders, however, if winter is not in fact their most colourful season. Many trees have been chosen for special bark, a backdrop for the hellebores.

Saving and Sharing in the Pyrenees

Marie-Joseph Teillard started her garden at the Château de Momas near Pau in the Pyrenees foothills in 1984. She says now that she undertook the restoration of the château as she might have entered a convent, with the preservation of a fast-disappearing regional heritage as her vocation. Not one, however, that precludes acclimatizing exotics, especially those finds that had been 'introduced by local nurserymen in love with their work'. 'Collecting is a passion like another', she says simply. 'Some people prefer fishing. It is my drug – it costs as much but is better for my health. But I always want just one more little flower.'

Saving and sharing have become Madame Teillard's whole life. Until retirement, she worked in an insurance office in Pau but never forgot her childhood garden in Lourdes. The property she chose was a dilapidated manor house on the edge of a village of some three hundred souls at an altitude of nearly two hundred metres. A feudal keep existed on this mountain outcrop as early as the tenth century. The present house, with its speckled-grey pebble-and-mortar walls and rust-toned roofs, was begun in 1343 and occupied

by the same family until the Revolution. When Madame Teillard arrived, the gardens were overrun with brambles, but she restored them according to the plan remembered by one of the château's surviving gardeners. She recalls that she quickly got 'clipper elbow'.

If she could do the job single-handedly, Madame Teillard would save all the local farms, country crafts and mountain landscapes that she now sees being planted with 'Alsatian Christmas trees' and Corsican pines. But she is not a purist. Quality and diversity go hand in hand for her. She remembers with pride that her own great-grandfather, a botanist and a pharmacist, was admired for his introductions of medicinal plants from Puerto Rico.

Sharing for Madame Teillard takes the form of biannual plant fairs: in the second week of April for perennial flowers; and for local fruit trees, she chooses the weekend closest to Saint Catherine's day (November 25), when, as a French proverb has it, all wood takes root. But sharing also means growing coriander for a neighbour who supplies the Chinese restaurants of Pau with baby sweetcorn, since his customers insist on having this 'Chinese parsley'. Or learning from Gilbert, an old Pyrenees gardener, how to prune

At the Château de Momas, large, venerable trees create a dappled shade, under which both Madame Teillard and her beloved plants thrive.

her almond tree when it is already in leaf because springs are unpredictable in this climate.

The garden at Momas slopes down from the house, but wears like a fringe on the horizon a long range of mountains, especially the Pic de Bigorre opposite the house entrance. On this sloping ground, two barns and an old well add height, as do tall shade trees: ash (common in these parts), horse chestnut and lime. The soil here is chalky clay. Low beds of perennials and shrubs edge this more-open, grassy space, and also climb up steps to a raised terrace by the front door, where shrubby veronicas are half smothered in variegated nasturtiums.

Around the rustic well at Momas cluster evening primroses, tender but dazzling tibouchina and the late-blooming bulb *schizostylis*.

In the shade of ash canopies grow the delicious vanilla-scented *azara*, rising from the pale pink flowers of *Centaurea largatissima* mixed with polygonum, day lilies, a small Japanese willow, and yellow and white phlomis. On one wall is the clematis 'Duchesse d'Albay', across the way from the 'Duchess of Edinburgh' variety: Madame Teillard likes to say that she has two duchesses strolling through her garden. By the small entrance path, she mixes shrubby salvias with yellow Pyrenees poppies, raimondia (also from the Pyrenees) and lamium 'White Nancy'. Shady foundations are planted with many camellias and hydrangeas, both cottagey and rare varieties, underplanted with a rosy coral, pale-pink-and-white mix of late-flowering *schizostylis*, and punctuated by a purple wisteria grown as a standard. Pale, potato-flowered *Solanum jasminoïdes* rambles over the potager barn but also reappears grown as a standard among the vegetables. The mood is always informal; the scale, always intimate; the air, always suffused with fragrance.

Madame Teillard acquires her plants from many sources, trading as much as buying. But when she brings back subjects from commercial nurseries, she always shakes all the earth off the roots, repotting them and nursing them for a season before setting them out in her own ground. Too many producers, she complains, use enriched potting mixtures that hype up the plants so that they die in ordinary conditions. She does almost everything herself, in spite of being nearly eighty and subject to sciatica. Sometimes, she takes on part-time help, jobless youths who, though full of goodwill, may run over hoses with the lawnmower, or dig up all the perennial geraniums as weeds. One of her daughters comes from Pau on weekends, to help with the cooking (which her mother neglects) and with the dogs, cats and poultry.

Her potager lies on the lower, south-eastern slope, which still has a mountain view and is accessible beyond a low stuccoed wall through a small wooden gate. Its beds are laid out anew each spring in long narrow strips separated by flat stones, connected by grass or a few cement-pebble paths. Madame Teillard believes in interplanting to protect crops: marigolds mixed with red-ribbed chard fight carrot-fly, for instance. Tufts of comfrey and nettles regularly provide their foliage for the maceration of plant sprays that will both nourish plants and protect them from insects. Marie-Joseph also grows seeds for the birds, and puts out wood for hedgehogs.

Among her treasures are the climbing 'strawberry spinach' (*Chenopodium apitatum*), long Armenian cucumbers, Mexican and Peruvian physalis (she loves their lavatera-like foliage as well as the Chinese-lantern fruit), white eggplants eaten when tiny but allowed to grow to the size of footballs for propagation. There are also an oenothera known as the 'ham of the poor', square peas and vineyard leeks. These produce cloves like garlic, which Madame Teillard says make lovely gratins in a white sauce. Local fruit varieties such as Golden Drop figs and Roussane peaches grow next to Pineapple guavas and Nashi pears from Japan, or the kawai, a hairless kiwi plant, which she strongly recommends, now threading its way through an old apple tree. Kiwis, she explains, will ripen if you put them in a paper bag with apples. She learned this from a nurseryman near Pau, just retired, whose extensive collection included both pink and green ones.

She seeks out the rare and beautiful, whatever its origins, pursuing the goal of biodiversity with energy, knowledge and imagination. She can tell you everything about King Henri IV, a hero of the Béarn region, who was famous for promising a chicken in every pot on Sundays.

The richly endowed kitchen garden at Momas contains many rare vegetable varieties intermingled with country classics such as dahlias.

A well-known stuffed cabbage dish traditionally accompanies the king's legendary stew. Madame Teillard now prepares the dish with Pe-Tsai, or Chinese cabbage – lighter, she finds, than the old local country varieties.

Madame Teillard is exceptional in her energy and knowledge, but not in her enthusiasm. Plant fairs like hers have been started all over the country by people who seek, as she does, to preserve a local heritage while entering, with the plant-hunter's typical curiosity, into an age of global gardening.

Heirloom produce

Madame Teillard asked nurseryman Monsieur Larrouy about the apples of her childhood. He pushed back his Béarnais beret and said, 'You mena you don't want Goldens?' They found varieties with names like 'Pay bou' ('good father'), 'Mus de lebe' ('hare's muzzle') and 'Sang de boueilh' ('bull's blood'). In her potager are the celebrated white beans of Tarbes, used in cassoulet, the famous Japanese chestnut pumpkin, or potimarron, and christophines grown on strong posts and wires with sweet potatoes at their feet. When the christophines are ripe, Madame Teillard explains, they stick out their tongues, showing a little slip.

Collecting as a Fine Art in Picardy

La Verderonne in Picardy, some fifty miles north of Paris, exemplifies a plant-collecting style in which aesthetics take the lead. Like the gardens at Bellevue, La Verderonne offers an excellent example of the trend towards presenting unusual plants in a sequence of spaces, each with a different character. But whereas at Bellevue the spaces are created to fit the plants, here the plants are chosen to blend with an existing and distinguished architectural ensemble. The whole complex covers roughly one hectare. Restoration and planting were begun energetically in the mid-1980s by Dr Henri Cassoly and his friends and partners Marie and Guillaume de Panafieu.

Dr Cassoly's grandfather was a horticulturist in Cannes, and he remembers a childhood garden near Toulon. As a practising physician, he went to sea with the French navy for five years and once again on dry land, he was determined to settle in a place where he could see water from his windows. Today, he lives at La Maison des Hirondelles (Swallow House), once the dairy of a nearby château, a long, narrow building with a picturesque lake extending all along the north side. The

Most separate gardens at La Verderonne can be glimpsed from those next door through a gate or a gap, or over a low bridge.

Panafieus have restored the former stables on the other side of the broad southern courtyard. The château itself remains in other hands, but these outbuildings are exceptionally elegant. They include a dovecote tower, a *pédiluve*, or long, sloping trough in which horses were once bathed, a small eighteenth-century theatre, and a wonderful nineteenth-century greenhouse, just reglazed. After nearly a hundred years of neglect, and fifteen or so years of restoration (still ongoing), La Verderonne has become a centre for the arts, with exhibits and concerts all summer long.

Though each space has its own scale and character, the whole derives much of its harmony not only from the soft brick, stone, stucco and tile of its several buildings, but also from a kind of fluid assembly of its parts. Most separate gardens can be glimpsed from those next door through a gate or a gap, or over a low hedge. The landscape around encircles without enclosing – woods across the lake, a quiet country road, the façade of the château itself as a romantic backdrop. Linking is accomplished also by the extensive collections of rambling roses and clematis that are often intertwined throughout the garden – for example, 'Vyvyan Pennell' with the rose 'William Allen Richardson' on the façade of Swallow House rising from a cloud of phlomis and peach-leafed campanulas. These plantings are part of a broad border with golden tones dominating, including the roses 'Buff Beauty' and *Rosa chinensis* 'Mutabilis', a *Cornus alternifolia* 'Argentea', self-sown *Cosmos sulphureus* and larkspur, and, for autumn, blue-flowered caryopteris and golden helianthus. Winter offers a thicket of white-blooming heather around a golden pine.

The enclosed Cutting Garden (*jardin fleuriste*) around the old greenhouse has proven one of the most popular parts of the garden, sometimes praised as a *jardin de curé*. Dr Cassoly explains that the greenhouse, Dutch in origin, is unusual in having a rounded roof for better exposure with a walkway along the top. Around it are a collection of iris, a whole

Beneath the windows of Swallow House, a spiraea blooms happily under the laden branches of a rose named 'Suzy'.

wall of roses and clematis and semi-formal beds packed with perennials. Through a hornbeam hedge lies a much more open composition centred on a circular pool where golden tones again take precedence: day-lilies, honeysuckle, achilleas and rudbeckias, made light by tufts of grasses. Its small vegetable garden, where strips of salads are almost smothered by hollyhocks and asters, becomes one border among others, not a separate space. A new section under a tall beech and oak beyond the vegetables is being given over to a fern collection, mixed with ground-cover geraniums, tradescantias and hydrangeas purchased at … Martine Lemonnier's.

A narrow door changes the scale entirely as you emerge by the lake, with its two long borders, one under the house windows, the other stretching along the banks and in the water. Dr Cassoly takes particular pride in his shade-loving white-flowered *Chrysanthemum uliginosum* (syn. *Leucanthemella serotina*) which grows two metres high. At the end of the house, you cross a little bridge to rejoin the main courtyard.

How are choices made here? Dr Cassoly explains the planting of a new bed in the south-east corner of the courtyard. First, its shape, size and exact placing are determined with respect to the general structures of the garden (often underestimated, he feels). This space is circular to connect visually with the two round plantings already set at each end of the long border in front of Swallow House, themselves an echo of the nearby château's turrets. Next, he chooses the dominant colour – red here, since red appears very little in other sections. But it must be modulated with white flowers and silver foliage. Then the shrubs are selected: maples are excluded because of the alkaline soil. For evergreen foliage, photinias fit the bill: two 'Red Robin' for the strong red of

All the plantings at La Verderonne are artfully designed for harmony of tone and volume, with respect to the architecture of the nearby buildings.

their new foliage and one 'Serrulata' with more coppery tones. Then a purple-wooded willow (*S. purpurea* 'Nancy Saunders'), a *Prunus cistena*, some musk roses and a tall-growing eupatorium. For lower flowers still in red tones, he selects choice dahlias and lobelias, heuchera and epimedium, and for white contrasts, a double-blossomed *Hibiscus syriacus*, four *Hydrangea arborescens* 'Annabelle', exocorda, *Lavatera* 'Mont Blanc' and *Achillea* 'The Pearl'. Silver foliage is provided by artemesia 'Powis Castle' and annual poppies which, like *Cosmos* 'Purity' and red atriplex, are allowed to self-sow. The whole mixture blends beautifully with old brick and weathered roof tiles nearby.

The method is that of any careful English gardener planning a mixed border, but the results are quite different in their looser arrangement. A visiting British journalist used words like: 'tousled thickets' where tall inulas and maclayas 'leap out at you'. Controlled self-sowing contributes a lot to the overall atmosphere: Californian poppies spread in the iris collection; elsewhere, oak-leaf lettuce, feverfew or Clary sage are left alone. Large perennials do seem just barely contained, and Dr Cassoly particularly admires the effect of a 'Constance Spry' rose backlit against a stand of *Stipa gigantea* among self-sown marigolds. The plantings, like the design, remain fluid, never static nor rigid, nor yet dramatic but always softly controlled and contained by the strong architectural framework, which, with its rusted frames and time-worn cobbles, exactly corresponds to contemporary taste. So does the humour apparent here and there – in the naming of the potager, for example, as the Apostle Garden because it has twelve strips. However rich the collections at La Verderonne, rarity is always an aspect of refinement.

Plant associations

Dr Cassoly takes pleasure not only in the infinite variety of flower and leaf for each species, but also in artistic combinations. He likes to mix foliage by analogy of shapes or by contrasts; and hues by subtle blendings, avoiding complementary colours, which he finds too brutal in combination. In composing his pictures, he tries, moreover, to provide some interest for each season. For example, in combining two great rambling roses – a 'Kiftsgate' and Rosa laevigata – he appreciates similarities in their flowers, but equally enjoys their different-coloured fruit in winter.

Architectural variety

Proportion and scale count in the plantings at La Verderonne. For example, along the front of Swallow House runs an old cobble-stone path. The border which accompanies it has been planted some distance back from the path, so there is no stifled feeling of being closed in. At the same time, this breadth leaves perspectives open in both directions. Each of the buildings is surrounded in a way that both enhances its volume and sets it off, while serving as a support for the collections.

3

CELEBRATION OF THE SENSES

'*Jardins des cinq sens*' ('gardens for the five senses') have multiplied in France in recent years, appealing because of their mix of formal elegance, pleasure and practicality. Contemporary adaptations of the traditional herb garden, they often favour medieval inspiration, blending esoteric symbolism with down-to-earth plant lore in gardens that are historically evocative, gently pedagogical and of relatively low maintenance. Both private and public gardens, they are often found gracing historical monuments. A number of provincial cities – among them Strasbourg, Limoges and Toulouse – have planted public neo-medieval gardens mixing aromatics with fruits and vegetables.

The most famous example, perhaps, is at the Château d'Yvoire near Geneva, where Alain Richert designed a beautiful Labyrinth of the Five Senses. He has since also created medieval-inspired gardens for the Château de la Guyonnière near Poitiers and the Château du Colombier near Rodez. Richert warns, however, against the common misconception of the medieval walled enclosure, the famous *hortus conclusus*, as a refuge from the world. In those times, gardens belonged to the Church or to the aristocracy and were very much at the heart of society. Richert's own work takes from the medieval heritage its mix of sensuality and symbolism, material and spiritual nourishment.

Aromatic plants appeal in sensuous gardens, like Dominique Lafourcade's, for their fragrance and for the tones and textures of their all-year-round foliage.

Ornamental vegetable gardening has become a central focus of the new sensuous garden, as demonstrated here at Cordes-sur-Ciel.

Renaissance château owners favour elaborate parterres on this theme. At Amboise in the Loire valley, designer Aline Lecoeur is using existing sixteenth-century outlines in her contemporary *jardin des cinq sens*. The Conseil général of the Centre-Val de Loire region has restored the elegant, turreted Château de Chamerolles as an imaginative museum relating the history of perfume, planting a formal garden inspired, like parts of Amboise and Villandry, by the drawings of the Renaissance architect Jacques Androuet du Cerceau. Such projects link their formal patterns and sensuous experience to the intellectual allegories of the time. A Romantic version at Ainay-le-Vieil in the Berry, Georges Sand country, uses semi-walled outdoor

rooms called *chartreuses*, once built for forcing fruit, to shelter a series of contemporary *jardins des cinq sens*.

Sensuous gardens can be made on a shoestring budget, however. One of the most impressive examples was designed by Monique Lafon at the Romanesque Gardens of Arconce in Burgundy. While she was still owner of a nursery called Fragrance, Monique wanted a reference garden to show her customers new plants and also to rehabilitate 'weeds' with forgotten medicinal or household uses. Arconce, which now belongs to an association, displays ever-growing collections on a series of small terraces around a 'scented cloister'. This is very much a garden for use: groups of visually impaired children from a nearby institute are encouraged to roll about in the mint beds to their hearts' content. Monique is a creative woman from whose lips tales and recipes fall like jewels from the mouth of a fairy-tale princess. She has even imagined a pastry cook's garden where the plants smell of coconut, caramel and peanut butter.

Jardins des cinq sens are a mainspring of the new green tourism, and are frequently pedagogical. The Delbard family, an enterprise famous for producing both rose and fruit tree varieties, opens its experimental garden at Malicorne in the Auvergne for public workshops, while its catalogue explains in detail the 'olfactive landscape of the rose'. Some gardens are designed specifically with children in mind, such as the charming Domaine médiéval des Champs, a restored fortified village in the heart of the remote Lozère offering medieval crafts and banquets. Indeed, all of France has in recent years been swept up in a movement to educate children – and adults – towards a new 'sensorial awakening'. The Semaine du Goût (Week of Taste) now held every October involves many top-name chefs, who teach schoolchildren to appreciate local products, including the joys of a perfectly ripe pear. But each season has its specialities: all summer long in the lavender country of northern Provence you can visit a great variety of herb gardens, learn to make your own perfumes, be cured by aromatherapy and eat lavender ice cream, all in one weekend.

Edibles, of course, play a central role in this trend. A survey conducted in 1994 concluded that twenty-three per cent of French people grow at least some of their own fruits and vegetables. French family kitchen gardens have always appealed to all the senses, but today taste is even more discerning. On small rural markets, weathered old farmers now offer their customers gourmet specialities like *potimarron*, or chestnut squash, as well as heirloom varieties – a diversity now seriously threatened by European seed-distribution regulations (*see page 146*).

Ornamental château kitchen gardens are more popular than ever: world-famous Villandry has developed a whole new programme of activities. In upper Normandy, Miromesnil, Galleville and Bosmelet offer luxuriant walled potagers, the latter especially rejoining contemporary design with its Rainbow and Discovery gardens. La Bourdaisière near Tours has an elegant tomato conservatory, whereas the Château de Saint-Loup near Poitiers is restoring an orchard of some two thousand fruit trees. Saint-Jean-de-Beauregard, south-west of Paris, remains the principal inspiration for many of today's home gardeners, and holds a famous fruit and vegetable fair every autumn.

Multisensual gardening implies multiple uses for plants, including medicinal and household applications. Near Paris, Milly-la-Forêt has become famous as the home of an interprofessional institute of medicinal aromatics for both industrial and individual use. The Museum Garden of Limeuil in the Dordogne, one young couple's labour of love, presents period re-creations of food-producing gardens, starting with the Neolithic age – a remarkable series. The Prieuré de Salagon in the Provençal Alps, a major centre for ethnobotanic research, has four beautiful gardens ranging in style from neo-medieval to contemporary, illustrating the rich history of plant use.

Jardins des cinq sens are easily adaptable to plots of all sizes for people of all backgrounds. The Mediterranean world offers especially rich models since historically the separation between ornamental and utilitarian gardening never took place in southern France as it did north of the River Loire. And in Provence, every garden is a herb garden.

Each aspect of Alain Richert's lower Normandy mill offers a different character, and each of its gardenscapes varies accordingly.

'The Country Green and Provençal Song'

Avignon-born designer Dominique Lafourcade takes inspiration from the Provençal green garden, which for centuries surrounded country properties in southern France. Direct descendants of Roman domains, and cousins to Tuscan villas, these estates have always mixed elegance with agriculture, pleasure with profit. Max-Philippe Delavouet, a Provençal poet, once wrote that, 'Art in Provence is always peasant art … Its finest works always keep a refined and rustic air.' The best new Provençal gardens perpetuate this approach, and Dominique Lafourcade's are foremost among them. Her gardens are now imitated all over the world as a model for sensuous country living, Mediterranean style.

She began as a painter. Both gardens and painting are in her family, she explains, and her mother still appears regularly to help at home, painstakingly but devotedly deadheading the irises and picking the strawberries. Only Dominique can clip the broad-leaf evergreens, however. Design for her is in the fingers and the nose, as much as in the eye. She prunes with hand shears to get a soft, smooth cut, and shapes are born under her fingers like sculpture from stone.

Dominique Lafourcade cleverly transformed the foundations of an ugly storage shed into a gracious pool beside the terrace of the house.

Dominique's husband Bruno is an architect who restores old properties in Provence. Their favourite common project has been a golden farmhouse set on some twenty-two acres in the patchwork of apple cordons and cypress hedging typical of the Alpilles hills. About a tenth of the land has been transformed into a garden. Its formal patterns deliberately echo the agricultural geometries all around them as much as the green parterres of the past. It is very much a garden for the five senses.

Everything in the Mediterranean begins with climate control. Provençal gardens have always mixed deciduous and evergreen vegetation to create microclimates which vary with the seasons for greatest comfort and pleasure. The site in this garden is unusual for the region: broad, flat and windswept. When restoration began in the early 1990s, the house itself was protected to the south by a row of majestic planes, and to the north by white oaks. It had lingered on the market because of an ugly tin storage shed, which the Lafourcades removed, transforming its cement foundations into a rectangular pool. The garden was then laid out with hedging which both protects against the fierce northerly mistral wind and creates secret compartments.

Today, the garden unfolds around a central canal that flows towards distant fields south of the house terrace. But it is also flanked by a whole series of smaller, sheltered spaces: an Italianate half-circle at the west end of the house; a grey-and-blue garden to the east; a rosemary-and-rose garden enclosed by an ancient vine; an intimate herb garden; a semi-formal potager with greenhouse and a fairy-tale garden shed; a formal 'Portuguese' pleasure garden with a small square pool for private dips and a garden house for siestas; and a *boule* garden, which pays playful homage to the shape of the sphere in both stone

and foliage. All are separated and defined by evergreen lines. Dominique's most recent addition is a herb-and-flower garden inspired by medieval cloisters, its walls made of climbers and laburnum trained on pergolas around a central fountain.

The southern sun is felt as much as seen – sometimes too much. The walk round this main garden is shaded in most of its parts, under long arbours east and west of the central rectangle. These allow changing viewpoints while affording cool shade.

Scent is present in the aromatic foliage of evergreens which brush against you as you pass. The plants which provide seasonal colour are also fragrant: wisteria, jasmine, roses. To these old-fashioned varieties Dominique adds many of her own finds. The ginger flower, for example, has a scent 'that makes you want to roll on the ground! That's what ginger's about anyway, isn't it?' she asks.

As for taste, edible landscaping comes naturally in Provence, where local aromatics, used in cuisine and for herbal teas, form the backbone of most gardens. The two long arbours are draped not only with wisteria and 'Lady Banks' roses but also with grapevines, to which kiwi and blackberry vines have been added. You nibble as you walk.

The potager is entered along a formal apple cordon similar to those of the neighbour's fields. These are Starkings, which Dominique appreciates both for their bloom and for the red colour of their fruit, less for their taste. She calls them 'strawberry apples' and has planted strawberries at their feet. Bold forms emerge among the vegetables: sweetcorn, trellised tomatoes and peppers, rhubarb chard, artichokes and climbing squashes wrapped around a tall

Lafourcade's 'Portuguese' garden offers repose and intimate bathing, with the gentle sound of trickling water and fruit to pick nearby.

74

wooden tower. Cardoons, traditionally used in Provence for Christmas cooking, make huge silver fountains.

A good deal of eating and drinking is customary in Provençal gardens, so much so that several outdoor eating spaces are usually part of the design, varying once more according to season and time of day. Here the latest spot for dinner is in the new 'medieval' cloister. A bit far from the kitchen? 'Everyone pitches in and carries something', says Dominique. Her ideal, however, is to pick, clean, cook and eat produce right on the spot in a matter of minutes.

Sound here is first notable by its absence: this is a very quiet place. But any Mediterranean garden makes a celebration of water. The melodious fountain on the rectangular pool in front of the house is activated by an aeolian pump at the edge of the potager, so that its water, here as elsewhere in the garden, is circulated without wastage. Bruno's tiny rowing-boat can just barely turn around in this pool, but its gentle motion offers a fresh perception of the garden from a different level. There remains room in the water, however, for a great number of very vocal frogs, a population that visiting herons cannot quite keep in control. Now a family of ducks adds its many voices to the chorus. They have become pets which even the dogs accept, even though, because of their foraging, the entire canal has had to be rebuilt.

The green garden in Provence was always essentially a style for family living rather than for show. Dominique has added a contemporary note of whimsy. All around are wild-flower meadows in which she hopes someday to erect metal cut-outs of rampant bulls. Animal motifs throughout the garden are often symbols for her, not merely decorative – stone frogs, ceramic snails, the serpent column of the Italian amphitheatre. They appear some-

In the Lafourcade garden there are many places to walk or to sit, to feel the sun and shade, to nibble, to sniff, to dip, to talk or to be silent.

times in her poetry. For like all truly creative people, Dominique cannot stop. She makes garden mosaics out of broken pots and bits of mirror, picks pebbles one by one from the Durance river-bed for paving, cuts wicker branches at just the right moment when they are still supple enough for weaving into picture frames and furniture. Hanging in her workshop is a quotation adapted from the Roman poet Horace: 'He who mingles use and beauty, simplicity and grandeur, will not have lived in vain.'

Colour and light

The bones of such a garden are clipped evergreen shrubs — box, laurustinus, myrtle and rosemary among them. Their squares and towers afford strong contrasts between sunlit and shaded planes. Not only do these large-scale compositions catch the light variously throughout the day and the year, they also create, with nearby cypresses, a beautiful play of shadows on flat, open spaces. Colour is provided by seasonal bloom against the range of green on green — wisteria and iris, roses, then large squares of scintillating lavender followed by lakes of brilliant perovskia. In autumn, vines and fruit trees turn red and gold, and in winter the laurustinus and rosemary are in flower.

Agricultural echoes

If the framework is formal, the design takes inspiration from farming landscapes. Here olive trees rather than oranges rise from the twin rows of Médicis pots. The canal itself was inspired by local irrigation networks. Dominique incorporated apple cordons using trees discarded by a farmer neighbour. Fields lining the long entrance road are planted with alfalfa for both decorative effect and soil enrichment, outlined with privet hedging. And if the house has been remodelled with a view to a symmetry typical of châteaux, its long, ochre-toned façade is still that of a local mas, or farmstead.

ALAIN RICHERT

Fragrant Meadows around a Mill in Normandy

Garden designer Alain Richert has been a painter, gallery-owner, calligrapher and film-maker, and now he teaches a workshop on 'Garden Art and Art in Gardens' at the École nationale supérieure du paysage in Versailles. His wife Catherine Willis is a sculptor specializing in olfactory effects. Garden design has become Alain's favourite medium because, as he once wrote, 'Paintings have no smell or taste and can't be eaten.'

In 1994, Alain and Catherine began creating, around an old mill in lower Normandy, a very contemporary garden for all the senses. It is not finished yet: Alain is working on a 'petal garden', inspired by old-fashioned small fruit plantings called *confituriers*, since Catherine makes preserves, creams and lotions from rose blossoms. But there is already a potager, an orchard, a pond leading to a shady stream, and a semi-formal hedged garden where Alain, the author of books on tulips and irises, experiments with new plant discoveries. Author also of a book on barnyard fowl, he cannot imagine a garden without birds. Opposite the house, a dovecote sends out its cooing, wheeling tenants, and the flight of

Alain Richert's wife, sculptor Catherine Willis, cherishes both scent and textural detail in this half-wild hedge meant to be seen close up.

these Damask doves has inspired Catherine to produce a sculpture series.

The long stone house and a weathered wooden barn on stilts are surrounded by sloping meadows. The canal that once fed the mill still runs nine months of the year under the house, linking a pond at the top of the hill to a stream at the bottom. Soil is poor and acidic. Tree belts of centuries-old oak and more recent hornbeam provide some wind protection, firewood and a massive, solid presence. A large field still belonging to a local farmer adjoins the Richerts' land by the road. But there are no obvious boundaries, and the garden gradually merges into rustic landscape.

Richert began, here as in all his projects, by establishing the routing of people and water – both of which are equally important to get right at the outset. The house remains central, but each of its aspects has a different character. Therefore, each of its gardenscapes varies also, both in scale and texture, within the overall harmony. The natural simplicity of the place is deceptive: its balance owes everything to Richert's careful planning and experienced eye. Perspectives remain multiple and shifting as you walk around.

In the Richert garden, too, sitting, feeling, enjoying fragrance, looking and reflecting are part of the pleasures of country living.

Wild flowers in grass and fragrant shrub roses link the garden's various parts. This mix begins only yards from the front door in the long strip which only half hides the vegetable plots, beyond the massive butcher's block which serves as an outdoor dining table. Catherine cherishes textural detail in this planting, which is always seen close up. Purple plantain intermingles with golden feverfew, a magenta geranium, *Euphorbia characias*, *Oenothera fruticosa*, wild digitalis and bronze fennel. Throughout the garden, colour choices favour purple and acid-yellow-green tones for everything that has no scent, but for perfumed species (in flower, leaf or bark) 'anything goes', says Alain.

Between house and orchard, the old pond stocked with multicoloured koi carp is lush with wetland plants. Alchemilla sets off wild herb bennet (*Geum*), the flowers of which are purple outside and yellow-green within. This makes an effective weed-suppressing ground cover near the Chinese willows *Salix fargesii* and *S. magnifica*.

On a much larger scale is the orchard, where mixed fruit trees rise between formal meadow squares. Their composition varies because of slight differences in soil and humidity. 'This is not really a meadow,' says Alain, 'not really a garden either, something in between.' Alain and Catherine add plants to existing grass, removing unwanted species. They favour cephalaria and various scabious along with knautia, geraniums, tansy and more alchemilla. A Pyrenees lily arrived two years ago only to disappear, but it is suddenly consenting to flower. Now Alain and Catherine are beginning to produce their own seedlings in a small nursery area. Asked why he planted wild flowers in grass around his fruit trees, Alain replies unhesitatingly: 'For the butterflies.'

Down the hill, past the west end of the house, rustic shrub plantings blur the garden boundary with a vast expanse of spontaneous meadow, white with daisies and red with clover in June, simply mown twice a year. The grassy path back to the house from the stream moves through a shadier planting of local trees and shrubs, woodland edging mixes of ground covers and bulbs. Emerging close to Catherine's studio, it moves past a ruin smothered in wild clematis, left there for birds to nest in.

Alain, always a plantsman, shows with pride a grouping of grandiflora magnolias by the wood, an old uncatalogued variety, he explains, which flowers very young in big blooms and stays only three metres high. He keeps horticultural treasures close to the house, with wilder and locally spontaneous species farther away – field maple or wild hawthorn, for example, so much of which has been lost either to rural zoning or fire-blight. *Cistus laurifolius* grows very well here, so he has added a lot of it to the tree belt.

International in his origins (he has Swedish, Swiss, German and Norman roots), and now creating gardens in many climates and under many skies, Alain always starts by exploring local conditions and resources. But he recalls that William Robinson, who has influenced his work, allowed exotics among native plants, even though he organized both with respect to local biotopes. Regional authorities have consulted Alain about the rehabilitation of their rural landscapes.

At first glance, the mill property might look like a 'natural' or enhanced landscape garden. Ecology and wildlife protection are certainly genuine concerns here. As early as the 1970s, Alain was convinced that the home garden offered the 'sole living model for the management of our environment'. But he insists that gardens are works of art created by human intervention. His designs are human-centred, not like those 'wild' gardens which seek to efface all traces of human presence. Idealism and practicality intermingle. Alain has only once designed a garden without edibles … a bare-earth garden for contemporary artists.

Earth counts a lot for Alain. He once observed with regret a man in the Paris metro carrying a bursting bag of potting soil from which everyone turned away in disgust. Bare earth is for him like the bare canvas often apparent in contemporary painting, or the spaces in calligraphy. Medieval gardens appeal to him for their harmony between earthiness and intellect, manual craftsmanship and 'high' art. In many of Alain's designs, wooden fencing illustrates this well: its different patterns create pleasing visual rhythms and textures; its placement establishes proportions and

spatial guidelines; its very presence is enclosing but at the same time invites the eye and spirit to pass beyond.

Detailing of this sort establishes balance with boldness. Nothing is ever static or settled. Says Alain, 'I chose this profession because it was the only way of pursuing all my curiosities at once.' He began decades ago with a natural meadow on industrial wasteland, but the mill garden is his first chance to put down roots into his own soil. It is both a compelling model for good country living and a subtle example of the best garden art.

Alain cannot imagine a garden without birds. The flight of his Damask doves inspired Catherine to produce a sculpture series.

Biodiversity

Variety and vitality blend here in many ways. Alain and Catherine take pleasure in mixing rare exotics with local wild flowers, moved by both botanical interest and ecological concerns. But the life of plants for Alain also means accumulated experience of other kinds: of friends who have brought cuttings, for example, or of a plant's own history — the rhododendron's trek from Nepal to Normandy, for instance. Thus the garden can be appreciated like a stamp album, where each individual element has its own story. Celebration of the senses passes through the imagination.

Magic Carpets at Cordes-sur-Ciel

Eric Ossart and Arnaud Maurières are well-known figures in the French gardening world: Eric was the in-house designer at the Conservatoire de Chaumont during the first five years of its existence (*see page 164*); and Arnaud was the founder and long-time director of the École méditerranéenne des jardins et du paysage in Grasse, and then designer for the Delbard family enterprise, producers of fragrant roses and fruit varieties. Together, this dynamic team created for the city of Blois its informal 'Jardin des cinq sens' and a rustic rose garden, where grasses and fruit cordons mix with flowers in monochrome displays of colours. In 1997, they took an unusual step for professional designers: they created their own public garden, renting 2,500 square metres of terraced hillside from the tiny municipality of Cordes-sur-Ciel, a picturesque village in the Midi-Pyrénées region.

Both men feel rooted in the Mediterranean, especially in the region's Arab lands. Arnaud's family lived for years in Algeria, and Eric was born in Morocco. They own a museum-quality collection of rare Persian carpets. But as well as displaying Islamic inspiration, the gardens at Cordes

Arnaud Maurières designs, while Eric Ossart is more the plantsman, but both love ephemeral creations like the kitchen garden at Cordes.

also echo the work of Brazilian landscape architect Roberto Burle Marx. Simultaneously medieval and avant-garde, Latin and Gallic, rustic and highly refined, these are, above all, very sensuous pleasure gardens.

The five senses are catered for right from the entrance of the gardens, with herbal teas and mixed-fruit cocktails, a basket of apricots and often conversation with the two creators, who will, if asked, also cook up a group meal. There are many shady places to sit and chat, a bookshop, Moroccan pots for sale and exotic plants to buy – unusual basils, for example.

The first garden, set on the entrance level at an intriguing diagonal to the path, is a kind of cloister tucked under the high stone street wall. Its roof and outer walls of rough chestnut posts support white-flowering gourds and fragrant moonflowers (*Lapageria* and *Ipomoea alba*). Black slate shards set in railway sleepers outline a four-part design, echoing monastery gardens with their allusion to the four rivers of paradise. A high planting on the upper retaining wall mixes striped miscanthus, buddleias, caper spurge, a rose or two and bright dahlias – the Mexican *coccinea* variety. A low border of *Elaeagnus* x *ebbingei* (powerfully fragrant in autumn) edges formal plantings, which include a rustic canna developed in

Cardoons are a magic, silver-foliage plant in the potager at Cordes, producing artichoke-like heads good for drying.

Lorraine around 1900 with the picturesque name 'touslesmois' (all months). It now grows wild in south-western France. Eric and Arnaud delight in plants that are considered vulgar by city folk but are found in old country gardens. 'Generosity counts more than good taste in gardens', says Arnaud.

Cymbalaria and sedums run wild on rough stone walls farther along the path, while a fragrant cloud of lilac and honey locusts hide the terrace below. As you turn the corner you suddenly see one of Cordes's most delightful features: a long staircase with a succession of galvanized-tin buckets extending along the ramp, each one spilling water over into the bucket below. All the water features here are playful and homey — extra large taps, for example. At the bottom of these stairs, hidden under the gatehouse, are three vast cisterns collecting pure spring water, which is then recycled throughout the garden. An amusing assemblage of copper pipes and more pails creates a pleasing musical trickle at all times. This is witty and whimsical garden sculpture.

The second level of the gardens offers another cloister with fountains, surrounded this time by a collection of very large-leafed plants (a semi-hardy banana plant *Musa basjoo*, pollarded catalpas, architectural *Sauromatum venosum* rising from a bed of variegated *Plectranthus purpuratus*). Opposite, stepping stones zigzag through a bright floral carpet, surrounded by live-willow hedging. Arnaud and Eric invented a technique for 'weaving' carpets with annual flowers. Half a dozen species are repeated in the same order in lines that continue around bends, never recurring with obvious symmetry. There are zinnias, giant ageratum, Queen Anne's lace, verbenas, salvias and, beyond, a late summer tapestry featuring deep-red and white dahlias, euphorbias, *Arenaria glauca* and frilly red-leafed perilla.

The bottom terrace, the largest, is mainly devoted to the experimental and highly decorative kitchen garden. The bank behind is planted with 'Lavender Dream' roses and dwarf lavenders, all very fragrant, mixed with giant garlic, lemon trees in pots and lemon-scented pelargoniums 'Lemon Fancy' and 'Mabel Gray'. Farther along, buddleias ('Lochinch' and 'Black Knight') have room to expand. The path itself is made of broken terracotta pot shards, not unpleasant to walk on, cracking and crinkling as you go. The vegetables are widely spaced and mulched with weathered straw (set outdoors for a year before use). A knee-high apple cordon edges the path.

The long staircase with its trickle downhill from bucket to bucket has proven one of the most inspirational features at Les Jardins des Paradis.

The itinerary now leads to a discreet and cool building, an intimate museum. Eric and Arnaud both feel that human constructions are essential in any garden. At Cordes, a new theme is announced each year: perfume in 1998, the colour blue in 1999. The outdoor plantings change accordingly, and so do the museum's exhibits. For 'blue' there was a textile collection illustrating the history of woad (*Isatis tinctoria*), the only naturally blue dye, produced for centuries in south-western France. The blue theme was also embodied in bright figure sculptures by a sculptor living in the Gard department, Michel Wohlfahrt. Scattered throughout the garden, these were mainly pairs of lovers who, according to an accompanying text, made love in the meadows at night.

The museum has several doors, one of which leads to a small cubicle lined with 'living walls' (plants set in wired felt and fed hydroponically), a technique developed by the famous green-haired botanist Patrick Blanc. Beyond is an elegant pool garden with a deck made from French-grown sequoia. Massive pots along its edge offer papyrus fronds, both American and Asian varieties. You can look back across the pool at the colourful vegetable display.

Always festive in their appeal, Les Jardins des Paradis also invite the public to participate in perfume and flower-arrangement workshops, tomato and apple tastings, and cut-dahlia auctions. October's Semaine du Goût offers delights such as black-radish ice cream and turnips candied with rose-water. The mood is pleasurable and lightly peda-gogical, typical of the new green tourism, while remaining one of its best examples. Witness the explanatory panels, one of the most difficult challenges in a public garden: here, they are discreet scrolls hung from rough wooden stakes, amusing and instructive, imaginative and not too abundant. People of all backgrounds respond with enthusi-asm, both to the welcome and to the whimsy.

The potager in paradise

In the heavenly cornucopia of the potager at Cordes can be found cardoons, 'Purple Teepee' beans next to 'Blue Eye' gladiolas, the hot 'Espelette' pepper famous in Basque cooking, earth almonds, plantain, variously coloured chards and fennels, collections of mallows and salvias, sixty-four varieties of tomato, some thirty other peppers, all manner of rare vines with edible fruit, and much else besides. A pergola of rough-woven chestnut shoots allows visitors to admire from comfortable shade.

The paradise plot

'Paradise' is a Persian word, explains Arnaud, meaning enclosure. And the two men use patterns inspired by cloisters, carpets and oases in their designs at Cordes, both to screen and to frame. The woven live-willow fence is allowed to leaf out only at the top to preserve transparency through its diamond patterns. The lowest terrace, both sheltered and open, has along most of its length a shady pergola from which the experimental kitchen garden can be inspected. Diagonals and zigzag paths throughout make small spaces seem larger. 'Paradise' also echoes the name of the town Cordes-sur-Ciel, since 'sur-Ciel' means 'in heaven'.

4

FORMAL PLAY

Formal gardens have affinities with both sculpture and architecture. Since the Renaissance, they have been laid out to complement nearby buildings, at first in opposition to the surrounding landscape, but later extending into it. Their creators were often credited with a will to dominate nature. Today, however, green geometries are often subverted by whimsy; forms are opened up and arranged in new combinations that never settle into solidity. This new approach no longer dictates any one particular direction to the eye or to the feet but is both playful and participatory. Some gardeners use diagonals that cut across squares; others play with surprises in scale. Symbolism, often closely related to formal patterns in historic gardens, is now more personal, fanciful or witty – as in the Magic and Alchemy gardens at the Mas de la Brune in Provence. Cerebral abstraction is made sensuous in a variety of ways.

Châteaux parterres were always designed for double viewing: along main axes as well as from upper-storey windows. Today's overviews may be from aeroplanes. In the early 1990s, Jacques Simon, a contemporary land artist, created many stylized field pictures that were visible only from the air, often on sites near airports. A European flag made from a blue rectangle of bachelor's buttons and a star circle of wheat is perhaps his most famous work. Simon

Nicole de Vésian had an architect's eye for the organization of volumes into planes and perspectives at La Louve in Provence.

Today's green geometries serve as a foil for seasonal variations of the most fanciful kind, as at Les Fournials.

takes his inspiration not from châteaux but from the geometries of agricultural landscapes, and claims that his favourite tools are the bulldozer and the helicopter. These two points of view, from within and from above, remain crucial and sometimes problematic in the new land art, so often recorded only from the frontal vantage point of the photograph. Similarly, home gardeners sometimes use a nearby hill or hummock to provide an overall view of the playful patterns of their designs.

Formal gardening often uses hedging – green walls – to create a series of green rooms. Even modest home gardens are enjoying the fashion for narrative sequence where each space provides a variation on a theme. Both the Albarède and Cadiot gardens in the Dordogne, for example, alternate 'natural' gardens with sculpted box compositions. Eric Borja's Rhône valley garden has been admired for its juxtaposition of Japanese and Mediterranean inspiration – 'Japanese' meaning here a blend of mineral and minimal; 'Mediterranean' suggesting green forms that seem almost sculpted by the powerful southern sunshine. In Provence, designers like Michel Semini create patterns with green globes and squares, while garden 'sculptor' Alain Idoux has left us with striking almond-tree spirals and lavender rivers, again linking with land art.

The epitome of the formal itinerary, both playful and participatory, is the maze, tremendously popular in France in recent years. One gardener began planting a small version when his son was two years old with the idea that the hedges would grow along with the child. Today, an association called Labyrinthus plants elaborate and beautiful corn mazes every summer on numerous sites, more and more each year. Indeed, formal gardens are among the biggest attractions of the new green tourism. Three recently restored or newly created château examples in south-western France are Hautefort (with a traditional parterre and a labyrinth), Eyrignac (elegantly elaborate green rooms and topiary) and Marqueyssac (six kilometres of promenade among hand-pruned box hedges).

In the new formal gardens, the gap between landscape architecture and plantsmanship has to some extent been bridged. Louis Benech, commissioned with Jacques Wirtz and Pascal Cribier to redesign the formal Carrousel and Tuileries gardens in central Paris, is not only an architect but also a knowledgable plantsman. On the other hand,

Gilles Clément, usually associated with 'natural' gardening, has frequently been asked to design formal spaces. In the city of Blois, his still uncompleted designs reflect the history and symbolism of the local château, as formal gardens often have done in the past. But on the lowest of the three terraces, instead of the traditional closed rectangles, Clément has played with parallel lines of green hedging. On the garden plan posted nearby these hedges seem to have daunting regularity, but seen in three dimensions, each one has it own contour. Together, they appear like a series of waves. Planted between them is a grandmotherly mix of small trees, perennials and even vegetables gone to seed, all airy and mobile (*see page 11*).

In private gardens, the potager has for centuries been laid out in formal patterns of lines and squares. Today, it provides a model for witty interpretations. Thus, Benech imagined a 'false' potager near an elegant Norman country manor: its dwarf-box rectangles are laid out in regular array as in a traditional kitchen garden, but are filled with perennials instead of vegetables. Cribier also played on the potager model at La Coquetterie in upper Normandy, where a long courtyard has been filled with thirty-six squares mixing shrubs, perennials, herbs and vegetables.

Home gardeners today have also revived the pleasures of topiary as a kind of contemporary sculpture. Monsieur Mausset in the Limousin boasts of having created ninety different forms. Even along mountain roads where box grows wild, workmen clearing roadside vegetation frequently prune fantastic shapes from their imaginations.

Clipped greenery also means mown lawns, more justifiable today as plant sculpture than as a foil for plants or as a filler. Formal geometries can be created with differences of level, slopes and planes, which can catch light variously throughout the day, especially when set off by pools. Cut-grass paths can also outline wild-meadow squares and orchard rows, as in several distinctive Norman gardens – for instance, Marc Brown's, Alain Richert's or the family nursery of Le Jardin Plume.

Above all, formal gardening in France today has erupted into playful patterning more for enjoyment than for restriction. There is a general lightening, sometimes through the mobility of water or through the use of more-transparent materials like trellising, rough-wood fencing and live-willow hedges. At the same time, within the solid permanence of green architecture (box hedges may last for centuries) many gardeners today welcome the ephemeral life span, colour and fragrance of flowers.

Existing architecture still participates directly in formal design, inspiring plant patterns in endless variety, as at Le Prieuré d'Orsan.

Clipped Character in Provence

Nicole de Vésian began restoring her Provençal terrace garden on the lower fringe of a medieval hill town in 1987. 'La Louve' ('The She-wolf') was the name of her small domain. Here the former fashion stylist designed house and garden in harmony with the natural surroundings, producing a result with the concision, beauty and elegance of a Frank Lloyd Wright prairie house. Carefully maintained since her death in 1997, the garden is still held in high regard, especially by Japanese landscape architects and fashion leaders, and it inspires imitators all over the world.

At the end of her life, Vésian preferred rough, rustic and elemental modes to glamour. She came to resemble her garden: her careful *coiffure* became slicked back; her face, burnished like old copper; her clothes, leather and linen echoing the wood, stone and tough-scented foliage of the Provençal garrigue. Before retiring to the south, however, she had had a distinguished career in fashion. In the 1960s, the media nicknamed her 'the career-girl countess'. Working out of both Paris and New York, she designed many things, from shoes and knitware to perfume packaging and the interiors of Renault cars custom built

Nicole de Vésian first began clipping in imitation of wind-cropped and wild Mediterranean plants. Later, she was inspired by Japanese designers.

for film stars. Her Paris studio, New Vision, was housed in a renovated coal depot just a few steps away from the Élysée Palace. Even in those days, however, she often surprised by her inventive simplicity. At her famous off-beat dinner parties, the centre-piece might be, for example, cheap pearls strung across a big red cabbage.

Whatever project lay at hand, its success depended on Vésian's remarkable visual sense. If formal gardening is first and foremost a question of spatial balance between volumes and planes, La Louve is highly formal. These medieval hill towns are already strongly architectural. Their contrasting horizontals and verticals resemble a game of snakes and ladders, repeating lines and forms, passages and panoramas, and yet completely without symmetry. La Louve, covering only five hundred square metres in all, encompasses these village geometries in its three-storey house, strips of terracing and high stone walls. It also includes agricultural patterning in its lines of lavender on the lower terrace. Although it appears formal because of its smoothly clipped greenery – globes and domes, curtains and tapestries – the tone remains rustic, rough and rugged. All the materials – plants, stone and wood – are worn and weathered, marked by the passage of time.

At La Louve, the steep retaining walls permit both enclosure and panorama. The long perspectives east and west offer a series of planes and volumes, full of hidden spaces and foreshortening effects. In the tapestry plantings, smaller patterns evolve among larger ones. Twin shrubs often mark transitions, like the two myrtles closely positioned so that visitors must rub against their fragrant foliage when passing. Vésian generally avoided bilateral symmetry, however. Above all, design at La Louve is always intimate, a sequence of small spaces.

This meticulous organization was never cerebral: Vésian found it impossible to work from plans. The first inspiration at La Louve, and in the handful of gardens she later made for friends, was always some feature of the surrounding landscape, perhaps a tall cypress or a group of trees, from which a vista unfolded. Her own garden was not designed as a place to relax but as a place for looking out, its many benches and chairs placed for best views, not for shady siestas or outdoor dining. Viewpoints in all her gardens are always multiple and criss-crossing, arranged without seeming contrived.

The house at La Louve, though central, was rebuilt to fit the garden, its windows cut to frame outside views rather than for inside convenience. Vésian imported local river pebbles to use both inside the house by the front door and for the outdoor kitchen terrace, instead of paving. Another strong indoor–outdoor link is the long wing she called the 'Winter Garden', a room with its fourth wall made of glass doors, usually open. Here, as in the garden shed, she hung slightly tarnished mirrors to reflect not the viewer but the landscape beyond.

Vésian's whole approach was architectural, and plant names remained a mystery for her. She made much of an evergreen elaeagnus with silvery-beige tones on the underleaf, which she affectionately nicknamed her 'ebbingies'. But plants grew for her, nonetheless: she would recuperate cypress trees that the nurserymen had abandoned, cut their tops flat to encourage growth and nurse them back to health. Flat-topped cypresses became a Vésian hallmark.

Clipped greenery traditionally signifies a desire to control natural growth, to impose architectural permanence on the accidents and evolution of biology. This

At La Louve, a pear tree blooms in a planter where rough local stones, cut and assembled with regularity, each keep their own character.

assumption is everywhere challenged in contemporary garden design. At La Louve, formal patterning incorporates much creative whimsy. In the long lavender field of the lower terrace, Vésian experimented with pruning only every second plant to create patterns seen from both above and within, transforming by the simplest of means a banal agricultural feature into a kind of sculpture. Inspiration here came from watching the games of two toddler grandchildren and imagining scale through their eyes. This approach implies a partnership with growth, time and change, a kind of playing with nature. Even inert matter can participate: a rusty barrel hoop simply hanging on a wooden peg against a stone wall was enjoyed for the changing shadows it made as the sun moved across it from hour to hour.

Few gardeners so readily welcomed chance and change. When flash-floods brought down a major wall overnight and broke off two fine yew trees, she repruned the remnants into cartwheel shapes and built a small balcony beyond for yet another viewpoint on the lower terrace. She had no problems with the unpredictability of growing plants, welcoming self-sowers (hollyhocks and even gaillardias). One cardoon became a giant fountain of silver foliage from September through to June. When it had to be cut down to the ground in July, she hid its vast absence by the expansion of surrounding plants, while saving its thistle heads for drying. Recycling all materials was never merely an economy for Vésian but a whole philosophy, her own way of letting the past nourish the future. Her garden was in constant evolution.

Indeed, the time came when she felt she had exhausted La Louve's possibilities and was ready to move on. The year in which she died, she purchased a flat, windswept site at the top of the village to begin anew. All at once she began to design her new garden, her new house … and the wheel-

Agricultural patterning inspired the lavender field at La Louve, where often only every second plant was allowed to flower, creating a sculptural effect.

chair she expected she would soon need. In the garden, only spontaneous wild plants were to be admitted, lichens and sedums on bare stone. But she was already clipping existing junipers and rosemary into clouds. She wrote in a diary not long before her death: 'I love liberty, space, light, harmony, balance, sobriety, creative activity, having time … I hate falseness, pretension, exaggeration, agitation. The most important thing in creating is independence, being capable of changing everything, at any time.'

Creative pruning

Vésian loved the wild aromatic plants of her region, where wind and drought have already created rounded shapes. Her pruning was not so much a taming of the local landscape as the establishment of a witty dialogue with the hillside beyond her garden. Her cistus, rosemary, box, laurustinus and dorycnium became globes, tapestries, families and assemblies, but never regiments. Each plant preserved its individual character while participating in the larger picture. Pruning served to lighten shapes as well as to create mass: the centre of an old strawberry tree was opened up to show off its reddish bark.

Rock and stone

Just as spontaneous vegetation becomes garden sculpture, so the rocky cliff outside shelters dry-set stone walls and the smooth stone globes that punctuate the garden. Landscape and garden are a continuum, not an opposition. The Luberon's pale limestone is a perfect foil for the evergreen aromatics. As a result, if some visitors see La Louve as formal, others consider it a wild garden. For some, it is quintessentially French; for others, it is Japanese or pan-Mediterranean. All agree that it is Provençal, however, a concentration of its immediate surroundings.

Wooded Whimsy in the Berry

The priory gardens at Orsan, fifty kilometres south of Bourges in the Cher department, were begun in 1991. Two young architects imagined this self-contained world, and started on a shoestring budget. Patrick Taravella (known as Tara) and Sonia Lesot decided to leave Paris nearly ten years ago and looked around in the wildly beautiful Berry province. Both had rural roots but Parisian experience; both wanted a garden that would be at once spiritual and sensual. Despairing of finding the old monastery of their dreams, they managed to purchase a U-shaped complex of ruins on some forty acres of land. The condition of the buildings was so bad that they got the entire property for the price of a studio apartment in Paris. 'It was fate that brought us to Orsan', says Sonia. 'When we began to study its history we found that we had bought a monastery after all!'

For when Tara and Sonia cleared away the debris, thanks to a tractor lent by farming neighbours, they discovered the ruins of a priory once dependent on the famous Loire abbey of Fontevraud. Founded by Robert d'Arbrissel in 1107, this was an original religious community to which both sexes were admitted, the men

commanded by the women. Today, massive stone and turreted buildings dating from the twelfth and seventeenth centuries serve to anchor the whole complex design, but the gardens dominate, far more than in medieval times. All of their square or rectangular 'rooms' are partially enclosed in hornbeam hedging. Each compartment has its own definite character, both symbolic and strikingly visual, highly formal but welcoming and intimate.

After a disastrous experience with a local designer, Tara and Sonia decided to forge on with their own ideas. Fate again intervened in the shape of a gifted gardener, Gilles Guillot, who came asking to join their enterprise. 'It was a marvellous adventure,' recalls Sonia, 'he took a great risk.' When the regional council offered a generous grant, expansion followed apace. Today, Gilles has two assistants to help him.

Tara describes their approach to garden design: 'Structure first and foremost. Once this is established, most of the work has been done. When Louis XIV decided to plan an axis linking the Louvre to his château at Saint-Germain-en-Laye, he made the Champs-Élysées ... and everything fell into place around this. Start with a strong structure, the rest is simple.' The couple has now created gardens covering

Wheat and other grain crops are used for formal effect at Orsan. They are mowed in squares and rectangles, and allowed to grow to different heights.

roughly five hectares, each space being first outlined, then filled in. New bee and dove gardens are in the planning stages, as well as guest-rooms for bed-and-breakfast visitors.

This is very much a contemporary fancy, not a historic restoration. Modern techniques are allowed for mowing and watering, though the soil is still worked manually in garden plots. The garden's colours are probably more subdued than in medieval times, just as the interiors of old churches are today admired for their natural bare stone, whereas medieval churchgoers once admired multicoloured frescos. Some of the original names for spaces have been kept, such as the infirmary, the fairground or the tile factory. But instead of the monks' refectory, for example, there is a small restaurant and tearoom where Tara has discovered a new vocation as a cook. 'Everything edible that is grown at Orsan is picked, dried, sold or prepared for our table or preserved', he says, proud of a cycle of growth that is both frugal and plentiful at once.

This utilitarian bias keeps plant interest as rich and diverse as the design variations. All of the Orsan plants can easily be grown by home gardeners and none are really rare. There are fifty-two different medicinal varieties in the four beds of the herb garden alone, including an unusual yellow-blossomed comfrey. The square fountain sits among four rectangles of Chenin blanc grapevines, from which a honey-flavoured white wine is made. In each corner is a woven wooden bench sheltered by a pruned-quince roof. In front of the main building are formal parterres presenting man's earliest food crop: three old varieties of wheat, rye and fava beans, all growing to different heights. The rose garden is dedicated to the Virgin, and is composed of two cloister-like enclosures, their ogival arches created by carefully clipped

Hornbeam hedging at Le Prieuré d'Orsan provides a solid formal frame for roses and overspilling lavender.

plum trees. One square features pink ramblers ('Cécile Brunner' and 'Madame Caroline Testout' among them). The other is all white ('Aimée Vibert' and 'Reine des Belges'). But the pink arches shelter white standard roses ('Iceberg' and 'Gruss an Aachen'), while the white arches contain pink ones ('Cornelia' and 'The Fairy'). Each of the climbers is carefully taken down from its supports for pruning every winter, then lovingly replaced, its branches bent to produce more flowers.

The kitchen-garden maze also has walls of plum cordons – greengage, Nancy and Saint Catherine varieties – to provide solace for those who lose their way. Its design provides just enough challenge, each turn leading to fresh angles of vision and new vegetable discoveries. The fruit avenue nearby is one of Orsan's prettiest features: espaliered gooseberries, raspberries trained between wooden rungs, bush blueberries shaded by branches on more wooden supports – so many patterns and textures, smells and tastes. The main orchard, once the monks' cemetery, has kept three ancient pear trees. Its green grass is said to be a symbol of heavenly bliss, an evocation of eternity both wistful and playful.

Sonia and Tara have also made connections with the outside landscape in a manner which is both medieval and highly contemporary. The ancient flowery mead is now a wild-flower meadow – 'idealized countryside', says Sonia, mindful that farm life was in reality often harsh. Mindful also that, while medieval monasteries shut out wild nature as unredeemed, today it is considered beautiful. The woodland at Orsan has become an outdoor sculpture gallery, sheltering one year, for example, an exhibit by seven different artists on the theme of Jacob's ladder. An outline of the former convent buildings has been mown in the rough grass.

The first visitors came to the garden in 1995. Today, they visit from all over Europe, despite the remoteness of

Even wisteria at Orsan is directed to fill just the right volume on the façade, naturally and gracefully but with careful control.

the site. Sonia feels strongly that this garden is very personal, a private creation which they share with visitors. She herself often presides at the entry, although they now operate with a small and dedicated staff. 'But because we have been so successful,' she says, 'people sometimes refuse to believe that I am the owner and not just a ticket-seller. One woman said, "My poor dear, it's going to your head!" Another swore she had seen the "real" owners arriving by helicopter.' It is difficult for the public to credit that such an ambitious undertaking has been so successfully realized by these talented young people with few resources other than hard work and imagination. The result is formally beautiful, deliciously sensual, full of magic, and one of the most original new gardens in France today.

Wood works

The Berry province is famous for its chestnut wood, which is supple and pest-resistant. Tara studied medieval miniatures to get inspiration for the rough-wood gloriettes, arches, woven fences and supports of every description which now mark the design at Orsan so strongly. 'We quickly found', he recalls, 'that these were artists' visions, impractical as working scale models. They had to be interpreted and adapted.' These structures define spaces, lines and planes in the way of formal hedging but with a much lighter effect, creating separation and enticement, mystery and invitation.

ERIC OSSART AND ARNAUD MAURIÈRES

Green Rooms in the South-West

Les Fournials, the private garden of Arnaud Maurières and Eric Ossart, lies in a tiny hamlet in south-western France. The Jardins des Paradis they created at Cordes (*see page 86*) were intended for public visits; but Les Fournials is an intimate refuge, a home garden in the truest sense. Here, however, the formal patterns are made up of straight lines and right angles, not the playful zigzags commonly used at Cordes. Movement comes from exuberant, varied and imaginative plantings within this formal framework.

They began in 1992 with an abandoned stone farmhouse, set across the road from a medieval church on a hectare of wild ash, oak and brambles. Today, only a burnt-orange stucco wall is visible from the road, mildly exotic though its hue echoes the colour of the steeple trim opposite. Its green door leads to a cool corridor shaded by a high-reaching Judas tree and an unidentified but truly rambling rose. This is the first of two main vistas, a straight axis from east to west along the house façade. Its high southern wall supports spilling vegetation and above, out of sight, the main garden. The far end of this first axis is flanked by two pairs of burnt-

As in old formal gardens, Les Fournials offers a high, all-embracing viewpoint, here from the roof terrace of the house's modern extension.

orange walls framing sunlit fields beyond, an effect echoing the work of Mexican architect Luis Barragàn. Their austerity contrasts pleasingly with the cottagey profusion of the recessed wall planters and other homey details, such as a weathered stone well with a gargoyle downspout, a long wood pile, a worn wooden table and two chairs.

The garden's second main vista runs perpendicular to the first, starting from the juncture of the old farmhouse and the modern extension and emerging among oak trees near a communal path. Along most of its length, it is accompanied by high hornbeam hedges. Green rooms of different sizes open left and right through doors cut in the hedging. The control of space and perspective is so subtle and so complete that, from within, the garden seems much larger than its 1,200 square metres. By walking merely ten metres in any direction, you can change moods and views entirely, moving from the entrance courtyard to a wild-grass garden, an apricot garden, a section with formal twin pools and another with twin 'forests' of rare and fragrant shrubs under oak trees.

The whole design is both linked to the landscape and set apart, an effect achieved by restructuring the terrain at the outset. The house already stands on a height, though under the crest of the hill, dominating the surroundings but protected. Earth scooped out to make the twin pools was spread to raise the general level of the site by some thirty centimetres. Outer edges south and west were then held up by low walls in local stone, soft lines which nonetheless play with geometrical forms, sometimes convex, sometimes concave. They blend but simultaneously mark boundaries with the immediate surroundings.

Out in the western meadow is a large kitchen and cutting garden, and its sloping hayfield will soon have a formally patterned orchard. Seen from the bottom of this meadow, house and garden look like a self-contained monastery cluster, with the church steeple seeming to rise from its midst. The Judas tree stands at the exact point of juncture between the raised garden, the larger volumes of the house itself and the massive stone church. Stands of old

Diamond window patterning provides strong lines against which natural shapes, like the Judas tree by the entrance, range all the more freely.

ash and oak trees anchor the masses north and south. From the meadow one can also see the single narrow vertical window, running two storeys high, of the modern addition to the house, another Barragàn effect but one which also recalls the archers' slits of medieval fortifications. It is rooted to the ground by a sun-catching square of barley, chosen for deliberate contrast of colour and texture. Another year this simple patch might be planted with cloudy blue phacelia, or turned into a mixed wild-flower meadow.

All these proportions have been carefully balanced, and yet symmetry is usually just barely apparent. One end of the north–south axis nearly gets lost in the grass garden. And if the perspective along these hedges frames idyllic farmland, the line has been bent slightly to focus on a small château. Deep inside the garden, there is almost a labyrinth effect: the western hedge, for example, suddenly angles right to disclose another hidden space, the apricot garden. As in traditional formal gardens, there is a high, all-embracing viewpoint, here from the flat roof terrace of the new addition, itself an assemblage of rectangles.

The garden's most formal feature is the pair of long rectangular pools flanking a square of green lawn. One is a shallow pond; the other, a deep swimming pool (a juxtaposition suggested by Lawrence Johnston's Riviera garden at La Serre de la Madonne). From the nearest pool, sunlight playing on the water reflects on the ceilings within the house – an effect inspired by the Moorish gardens of Granada.

Like Nicole de Vésian, Eric and Arnaud restored the house to fit the garden. Old and new elements are carefully blended: the old part has kept its rough stone walls and slate roof but has lost its shutters; its windows now have a diamond-patterned iron grating. The new extension to the west – more burnt-orange stucco walls – keeps its simple rectangular forms, but some of its openings repeat the diamond motif in open tilework, a design the pair discovered in the tobacco factories around Granada. Using grillwork instead of shutters means that the garden is always visible. Windows are practically at ground level, especially in the modern part, where, just at teatime, the high slit lights up an indoor fountain surrounded by cushions. Inside the house, the décor repeats many patterns and colours from outside, but with no house plants: 'Carpets indoors, plants outside', says Eric.

Each of the upper-level windows offers a different view, culminating in the roof terrace at the far west end. From here you can also discover that the orange boundary walls hide another small building, with an undulating plastic roof looking from above like a white rectangle. This serves at ground level as a most discreet garden shed and greenhouse, almost invisible from the garden itself.

Within these controlled geometries, the plantings seem like so many little corners of managed wilderness. The vegetation itself is carefully chosen for scent and texture as well as for colour, combining the local and the exotic, and even some rarities. In their work all over France and North Africa, Eric and Arnaud have specialized in 'carpet' designs of colourful annuals, but they have also created 'nomad' gardens and land-art assemblages – both of which are approaches that create formal patterns with ephemeral materials. The result is a fine blending of rustic tradition and avant-garde formalism: the geometries of agriculture and of contemporary art combined. Above all, both in its design and its textures, Les Fournials echoes Barragàn's ideal of a garden as 'a magic place for the enjoyment of meditation and companionship'.

The spikes, masses and tones of pampas grass make an unusual winter picture with bare fruit tree forms and spear-like sculpture.

Walls and hedges

Height confers a third dimension to the 'carpet' geometries particularly favoured by these designers. Eric Ossart wrote his thesis for the École nationale supérieure du paysage in Versailles on the subject of walls, which he uses for framing vistas and terracing as well as for enclosing. Walls can also be screens for the projection of shadows and reflections, echoing the sky. As for the hornbeam hedges, they are deliberately perpendicular to prevailing easterly and westerly winds, combining practicality with formal elegance. 'And they all lead somewhere', says Arnaud proudly.

5

NATURE'S WAYS

'Natural' gardening in France today covers a lot of ground, so to speak: a 1999 *L'Express* magazine survey revealed that this style was the favourite among French amateur gardeners. For some, it means wild-flower gardening, creating less formal, more spontaneous-looking plant pictures. For others, it means preserving local landscapes and ecosystems, cherishing and enhancing a characteristic bit of countryside for its very own 'spirit of place'. And for a growing number of gardeners, it means achieving a communion with nature through the new land or earth art. Motivation is both aesthetic and ecological. As landscape artist Bernard Lassus puts it, 'Water must be clean and we must be inventive.'

Although idealized countryside can often be the first inspiration, natural gardening traditionally imitates wilderness, with a Romantic emphasis on the picturesque. France, industrialized late, still has many remote, sparsely populated regions of woodland, mountains and deep river gorges, and today 'wild' gardens proliferate all over the country, especially in the Massif Central, the whole of the south-west, the Rhône-Alpes region and Haute Provence. Some extreme of local climate may inspire the gardener: the Berger family's water garden in the Auvergne, for example, with its mill stream, cascades and small lake rich with wildlife; or the stony, bone-dry botanical garden of a

At La Roseraie de Berty in the Ardèche, an 'Adelaïde d'Orléans' rose stretches over a stream-bed, dry in summer, to form part of a wild mountain landscape.

Wilderness settings readily inspire land, earth or nature art, such as Erik Barray's *Blue Labyrinth*, set in a dense pine thicket at Le Vallon du Villaret.

descendants still imitate 'natural' landscapes so skilfully that the visitor may ask sceptically, like Rousseau's hero, 'Where is the garden?' Today's gardeners still practise the techniques the writer recommended to create their illusion: choosing self-sowing plants with both foliage and seed interest, grasses, mixed shrubs for rustic hedges and climbers for jungle effects; shunning straight lines and right angles; and arranging internal circuit watering to create 'natural' cascades.

Rousseau wanted a garden that was seemingly untouched by human hands. Paths and even houses were therefore embarrassing intrusions. In France today, however, 'wild' gardeners seek to deny the human presence much less than Rousseau would have liked. After all, other animals make habitats and paths, as one natural gardener points out. Landscape architects even experiment with 'palimpsest' gardens, where layers of history – both human and natural – are incorporated into spatial design. Jean Kling, an architect in the Orléans forest, has one solution: he has allowed his house to be smothered in vegetation, with a turf roof and a bit of lake running through the basement. If classic French style and industrial exploitation both assumed man's domination of nature, and if Romantics sought, on the contrary, to lose themselves in nature's immensity, modern natural gardeners seek responsible partnership. To paraphrase American writer Michael Pollan, the time for both the rape and the worship of Nature is past – the new ideal is marriage.

More common than wilderness, a French landscape model is the *friche* – farmland abandoned due to economic pressures. A survey published in *Le Monde* suggests that these lands attract three main groups: developers, hunters and ecologists wanting potential reserves for biodiversity. Human intervention is necessary to maintain the *friches*, however, even for conservation purposes, since abandoned

visionary shepherd in the Var, Elie Alexis. Top professional designers such as Camille Muller and the Breton Erwan Tymen have specialized in this style.

The great French celebrant of wilderness was, of course, Jean-Jacques Rousseau, whose fictional garden in *Julie, ou la Nouvelle Héloïse*, published in 1760, provided a model to many. Like 'Capability' Brown in England, Rousseau recommended creating an illusion of spontaneity, an artificial landscape with a convincingly natural look. Rousseau's land gradually becomes dominated by a single species, often by the dread conifers intolerant of other life. Maintained but uncultivated, *friche* can mean wild-flower meadows – a great garden model. Few new gardens are created in France today without a flowery mead, however small. Fine nurseries now specialize in wild-looking plants and grasses: for instance, Berchigrange in Lorraine, Les Jardins de Sauveterre in the Creuse, Filippi in Languedoc and the Pépinières de Vaugines in Provence.

Friche, not wilderness, was the starting-point for Gilles Clément's famous 'moving garden', first practised in his own home garden, La Vallée in the Creuse. Clément intervened just as his abandoned land reached its greatest diversity, experiencing this as a way of 'situating ourselves other than in terms of opposition between illusions of order or disorder. Watching wasteland I am not only fascinated by the energy of nature's reclamation, I also want to know how to insert myself in the midst of this powerful flow.' Clément recently proposed to city-planners an economical and labour-saving meadow model as a substitute for dreary *espaces verts*. Some of his students now have original semi-wild gardens of their own: Les Jardins de la Sedelle and Les Jardins de la Forge, also in the Creuse, are among the finest.

When wild nature is arranged artfully, it is but a step away from land, environmental, earth or nature art, where landscape becomes the subject and medium, not merely a setting. Since the 1970s, art centres like La Vassivière in the remote Limousin, or the Fondation Stahly in the Rhône valley, have offered international exchanges and works created on and for specific sites by such figures as David Nash, Andy Goldsworthy and Nils-Udo. The original land artists found living plants too unpredictable a medium, favouring instead mineral, inert or ephemeral materials, pre-

ferring decay to growth. Today, professionals and home artists alike connect natural process with garden art: the painted tree-stump sculpture of Les Jardins de l'Albarède in the Dordogne is a telling example. For these organic gardeners, nature's inevitable decay is merely part of its cycle. But so, with care, is regeneration, which, from the potted plant to the planet, is the concern of all natural gardeners.

Home gardeners like photographer Georges Lévêque connect natural process and garden art, accepting both growth and decay.

Home-Grown Ecology in a Loire Town Garden

❋

Home gardens today can offer an ideal partnership with nature. They can provide a refuge for biodiversity in the midst of suburban uniformity and, at the same time, an example of wise management of natural resources on a personal scale. Georges Lévêque and his family ascribe to both of these ideals. Since the 1970s, Georges has perhaps been France's most influential gardener as both photographer and writer for the leading magazine *Mon Jardin et ma maison*. His first inspiration was English, and his aims were above all aesthetic – Rosemary Verey soon became a model. Georges worked tirelessly for decades to increase horticultural awareness, to encourage young nurseries and designers, and to promote plantings that had an 'artistic dimension' but were within the means of the home gardener. The call of the wild was not unknown to him, however: he, too, dreamed of solar energy, of a natural marsh garden away from city life. For family reasons, he and his wife Françoise settled on a house on the main street of a small town between Paris and the Loire valley. Ten years ago, he began working intensively on his own very personal garden, a long, narrow plot behind the

In the Lévêque family garden, seed heads of fennel and poppy are considered as beautiful as flowers.

house shaded by high walls. Today, it successfully combines elegance and ecology, 'natural' beauty and sustainability.

The Lévêque family garden extends in a series of small spaces without formal transitions. Georges likes a long central axis, seen both from the house and from the other end of the garden where a small wood shelters and hides two parked cars. But many features interrupt this line, especially a second building built over a broad arch part way down, now housing Georges's home office. Changing textures on the ground also blur symmetry: from the house, the simple dirt path disappears under the arch in a mosaic of shade-loving plants, re-emerging as an irregular assemblage of old paving stones, before getting lost again in grass. Lines are also softened by the perpetual play of shade patterns cast by the many small trees and flowering shrubs throughout the day and throughout the year.

House and garden walls are smothered in near jungle-like growth of actinidia vines (inspired by the Arboretum de Kalmthout, and producing more than a thousand fruit), rambling roses ('Bobbie James' and 'Maréchal Ney'), a creeper on the house itself (*Parthenocissus Henryana*), espaliered cherry trees and a luxuriant Chasselas vine. One year, the latter got spots, but Georges refuses all chemicals, whether they be

Open parts of the garden have rough grass but not lawn. Unwatered and unfertilized, it turns dry and brown in summer.

working from a local biotope but welcoming selected introductions. By the house, *Impatiens balfourii* are prolific but easily controlled. Deep-pink poppies, yellow verbascum and feverfew self-sow throughout. The shade garden under the arch is very protected and gets a bit of water from holes in the roof, enough to support a low exotic garden of small broad-leaved evergreen shrubs such as *Ceanothus thyrsiflorus repens* mixed with sarcococcas, stephanandra and a plant that Georges loves, *Pieris* 'Little Heath Green'. Near the far end of the garden, a simple park bench lets the family enjoy birdsong in the tiny wild-flower meadow and woodland, composed of spontaneous yew and hornbeam that he has intermingled with raspberries, goldenrod, hogweed and eupatoria. In the wood itself, Georges welcomes spontaneous dogwood and snowberries, as well as a thick carpet of ivy. 'If I wanted to remove that,' he says, 'I would break all my tools.' So in March he simply cuts back all the woody stems close to the ground to enjoy new growth. Here and there he has inserted tough azaleas. 'This is what I call sensible ecology', he comments.

There are flowers for all seasons, all soft toned. 'I see so much colour in my work, I want something more restful at home', he says. He prefers foliage gardening, which is bright mainly in autumn. Leaves in a town space are, moreover, a means of purifying the air and combating pollution. In this sensuous garden, many plants are fragrant, like the *Rosa mulliganii* (formerly *R. longicuspis*) which cascades 'like a white tide' over an arch sheltering a small table and chairs. There is also a larger wooden dining table built by Georges around a majestic wild yew tree.

Open parts of the garden have grass, but not lawn. Few features of town and suburban gardens have caused as much controversy in recent years as energy-intensive turf, which ethnobotanist Pierre Lieutaghi condemned decades ago as

sprays or fertilizers. The problem cured itself. 'We eat half the grapes and dry half', he says. A small vegetable garden produces tomatoes, herbs and salad greens, but these sometimes get crowded out by cuttings of ornamentals. Wineberries near the house were a gift from Rosemary Verey. There are also pretty Japanese brambles with edible fruit (*Rubus phoenicolasius*) and a variety of apricots from the Tyrol.

Local, spontaneously sown plants intermingle throughout with 'exotics', the treasures which Georges brings home from his travels. 'Each region, each *terroir* has its vegetation,' Georges explains, 'you have first to be attentive to that. You start with what grows wild, the imports come after.' His approach is not unlike that of William Robinson in England a century ago, the outdoor equivalent of wall-to-wall carpeting. American writers are particularly scathing: Janet Martinelli complains that, 'Across a continent of breathtaking natural diversity, we've planted turf and petunias.' She remembers her father, in desperation, spray-painting a summer lawn green. Janet today chooses native American plants for her Brooklyn town garden. In France, too, lawns have consumed much space and energy. But as early as 1993 a gardening magazine for French railway employees noted that it was now acceptable to replace lawn with meadow mixes without upsetting the neighbours. Georges's approach is to encourage rough grass, which he cuts in May and June three times a week with a manual mower. Unwatered and unfertilized, it turns dry and brown in summer, greening again at the first rain. His miniature meadow is simply grass left to grow high, enriched with wild flowers.

Everyone in the family views gardening as a means of preserving natural balances. This includes fauna – three Sussex hens which commute in summer to their own vacation home, the compost pile at the other end of the garden. They come home every evening, however, 'hop, hop marching like scouts', says Georges, happy in this domestic complicity. The seeds they spread attract other birds, who thrive despite half-wild cats, also regarded as family friends.

This is a frugal garden, Georges explains, where hard work replaces expense. He feels that he has created a small corner of countryside in the heart of town, so secluded that you forget the bustle outside, but only a few minutes away from all the conveniences of urban living. How does one recognize a good garden? He replies: 'The house, its inhabitants and the garden must exist in harmony.'

Gentle woodland borders the Lévêque garden, where invasive periwinkle and wild ivy are appreciated, though kept in check.

Worlds within

This back garden of only a thousand square metres contains within itself many moods and many microclimates, from its grassy courtyard dense with rare witch-hazels and fruiting trees to the small mosaic-like shade garden under the arch, through to the sunny vegetable plots and picnic areas, ending in a small meadow and a bit of woodland, a parking space and the compost bins. Soft transitions, alternating sun and dappled shade ensure that there is no patchwork effect here, but a rare combination of harmony and adventure.

Old Roses in the Ardèche Wilderness

La Roseraie de Berty lies hidden in the heart of France. Two hours' drive south-west of Lyons, a winding, partially unpaved road finally ends in a mountain clearing. Here, a narrow gorge suddenly opens into gentle pastureland on both sides of a stream, then closes again abruptly – all at an altitude of about four hundred metres. This is chestnut-growing country, more austere than the sunny vineyards farther south. Winter temperatures can go as low as −10 °C, though never for very long.

Eléonore Cruse settled here in the early 1970s, choosing the site for the wild beauty of its steep wooded slopes dense with arbutus, box, bay and holly oak. Today, it shelters roughly six hundred species, varieties and cultivars of 'old' (that is, pre-1920s) roses. Eléonore has never counted exactly – with her partner Christian Biette she is much too busy gardening.

This is a collector's garden. The success of its design depends on an artful framing of each unique specimen in its context, never losing sight of neighbouring plants or of the stunning landscape all around. Eléonore and Christian are not trying to own 'one of everything', however. Rather, they have fallen in love with the colour, form,

texture, scent and motion of roses. Eléonore explains: 'What interests me most of all is art.' For her, there is no contradiction here with a love of wilderness – quite the contrary.

Eléonore began cultivating this site of roughly five thousand square metres soon after moving here. Like many young French people after 1968, she was aiming solely at self-sufficiency, with roses the last thing on her mind. Improvement came in several slow stages. The existing peach orchards had been both fertilized and weeded with chemicals, and the land was worn out. At first, Eléonore raised goats, Jersey cows and sheep, which cleaned up the terrain and enriched it. Then for two years she planted cover crops – phacelia, potatoes and rye – to get rid of perennial weeds. During this time, she learned to weave with wool from her sheep and to cane chairs with rye straw. After this patient preparation, she was ready to plant, and began with … vegetables. Little by little, she added rare plants for home-made vegetable dyes, with seeds from the Muséum d'Histoire naturelle in Paris, distributed as part of a programme to preserve disappearing species. Finally, intrigued above all by poetic names, Eléonore put a few roses among the green beans. 'If I had started with roses,' she says, 'it would never have worked, the soil was much too poor. But by the

The old farmhouse at Berty sits comfortably on terraces whose lines are now obscured by the tumbling of roses allowed to spread naturally.

time I got to them, it was rich and loamy.' Now, fifteen years later, she never uses fertilizers but only manure when planting new additions. She feels it is much more important to break up compact soil around the roots each spring than to feed.

Today, Eléonore Cruse is regarded as one of France's leading rose specialists, both because of her expertise in the field and her ability to design gardens around her cherished plants. She learned a great deal from rose producer André Eve of Pithiviers, and from gardening writer Michel Lys, both of whom have always generously supported young enthusiasts. First, Eléonore sold her favourites on country markets, then at the Marjolaine salon in Paris (the great mecca for French organic gardeners), and finally at the plant fair at Courson, where her reputation became firmly established.

Respect for nature determines her whole approach, including her methods of cultivation. She practises compan-ion planting with the many medicinal and aromatic plants that grow wild in southern France – sage, lavender, rosemary, thyme, all choices that look good with roses, while helping to protect them from diseases and pests. Sprays are kept to a minimum. Bordeaux mixture (copper sulphate) is applied at leaf-fall and when the buds swell. Sulphur is dusted by hand as a preventative measure in May, when the weather heats up during the day but nights are still cool. Only varieties known to be sensitive to downy mildew are treated. As a result, even 'Dorothy Perkins', 'Blue Magenta' and her 'Crimson Rambler' grown against a terrace wall rarely show traces of disease. By interplanting her roses with perennials and shrubs, Eléonore avoids the danger of monoculture that threatens any collection. Yet, in the densely planted islands which stretch enticingly across the valley floor, each rose remains clearly visible in habit and full flower.

The display of her many ramblers posed special problems. Perhaps her most original solution was the 'Ravine', a series of low arches spanning a mostly dry stream-bed, which displays ramblers right under the nose of visitors. But pruning is difficult. Long shoots have to be laid nearly flat and there is no footing below, so Eléonore may find herself finely balanced on a stepladder with a wire between her teeth. She does all the pruning herself and thinks it is a highly subjective process. Of course, Christian could do it, she says, 'expertly, but differently'. Each plant, not only each species, presents its own problem. 'You can't just count eyes as you do with a grapevine. Of course you have to let the light in, and above all simplify. Sometimes I cut back a lot, sometimes not at all. It depends also on how the roses relate to their neighbours, each rose must have its own space.'

Differences of level, soil depth and quality are turned to advantage: stone terrace walls protect tender plants in winter. Ground covers simplify upkeep while creating a natural flow between different parts of the garden. Some of the plants are common in the wild locally, while others are imported. *Tripleurospermum oreades* var. *tchihatchewii* (syn. *Matricaria tchihatchewii*) is a spreading, low-growing, turfy daisy. *Frankenia laevis* makes a good cover for the outer edge of terrace walls, always hard to keep clean. At the very feet of the roses, Eléonore likes *Viola tricolor*, wild pansies, perennial geraniums such as *Geranium sanguineum*, *G. psilostemon* and *G. grandiflorum*, *Tradescantia virginiana*, a wild, red-leafed epimedium known locally as 'elf ears' and *Phyla nodiflora* (syn. *Lippia*), a creeper which can even become too invasive. The tender, ever-flowering aster *Erigeron karvinskianus* loves the vertical surfaces. Wild strawberries spread sponta-

In the densely planted islands which stretch enticingly across the valley floor, each rose remains clearly visible in habit and full flower.

Three roses climb the wall of the house together: 'Zéphirine Drouhin', 'Alexandre Girault' and 'Albéric Barbier'.

neously in moist shade. The soil is very acidic: hybrid teas and the musk roses remain small in stature but flower well.

In stressing this natural look for a collection of roses, Eléonore Cruse has broken new ground. Traditionally, French rose gardens are very formal. It is true that André Eve began to challenge this style in the 1960s in his garden at Pithiviers, but Berty, vast in comparison, is not walled or set apart like Eve's. It is also far more remote, and open only in June. Even so, more and more people find their way there every year. Eléonore welcomes them in a tearoom with rose-petal syrup.

Designing with nature

The garden's outer edges blend into the natural landscape without clear boundaries. Below, the stream floods regularly, so its banks are left to rough grass, which is mowed twice a year and is resplendent in spring with wild orchids. On the steep land behind, wild arbutus, green oaks, laurel, cistus and heather require minimum maintenance. All man-made constructions use strictly local materials: bare rock peaking through sparse topsoil is echoed in the slate slabs of the house and the low terrace walls painstakingly rebuilt by Christian.

The artist at work

When designing a new planting at Berty or in other gardens, Eléonore starts by getting the feel of the place in all seasons. She imagines what colours and shapes would look best there, and has learned to keep in mind both the size and density of vegetation her plants will attain when adult. As for plant choices, Eléonore suggests experimenting with summer bouquets to test associations beforehand. In mixing colours, she works like a painter with her palette, sometimes enjoying definite contrast, sometimes creating subtle variations of tone in foliage and flower.

Nature, Play and Art in the Lozère

Le Vallon du Villaret covers ten hectares of woodland in the Lozère, one of France's most isolated and mountainous regions. Situated at an altitude of a thousand metres, it lies not far from a thermal resort, the Parc naturel des Cévennes, the source of the River Lot and the medium-sized city of Mende. At Le Vallon, visitors wind their way gently up one kilometre of the mountain gorge and then down again, zigzagging back and forth across a trout stream, and encountering works of art constructed especially for the site. These exist not merely to be admired but to be walked into, rolled in, smelt, touched, listened to – almost everything but eaten. A simple restaurant at the top of the hill looks after the palate. Nearby, a sixteenth-century tower offers indoor displays by leading contemporary artists. Studio space for visiting artists and an open-air theatre for summer concerts hide in the forest.

Le Vallon is advertised as an 'amusement park for children from two to seventy-two'. But can it also legitimately be labelled a garden? Nature, wrote Jean-Jacques Rousseau in 1760, flees populated areas, preferring mountain-tops, forests and desert islands. Gardens, according to this writer, are an artificial substitute for those who cannot travel to such faraway places and enjoy real wilderness. Transport has evolved since the eighteenth century, however, and in 1999 some 46,000 people found their way to Le Vallon, where Rousseau's categories of garden and wilderness converge. Guillaume Sonnet, the creator and moving spirit of the park, could say, like Rousseau's gardener, 'It is true that Nature did everything, but under my guidance.' At Le Vallon, a team of young enthusiasts maintains wilderness with complete discretion, yet evidence of subtle and creative human management shows up in every detail. Damp spots in paths, for example, are filled in with natural, local materials in such a way that planks, stone slabs and upright stepping logs rarely repeat the same pattern, becoming a visual game in themselves.

And then there is the large-scale art. In sunny open grassland you suddenly come across a terracotta toboggan. In a densely shaded stand of conifers carpeted only with needles, you discover a labyrinth of blue stakes echoing the tree trunks (the work of Lyon artist Erik Barray). The stream broadens here and there with natural stone patterning, a motif repeated in a curtain of sea shells hanging above it, moving in the breeze.

At Le Villaret, the *Land of Sounds* by Ivan Levasseur and Joël Vernier produces surprising effects when marbles are pushed through its orifices.

Even with numerous tourist coaches in the car park below, a visitor may feel serenely alone at Le Vallon. But the park is not meant to be Rousseau's solitary wilderness refuge: besides birdsong, you hear the intriguing chimes of Jean-Pierre Delettre and Michelle Elsair's *Water Mill* far above, and the floating laughter of children. Sonnet welcomes human beings as another, creative part of nature: a woman of seventy-nine went three times through the net bridge for sheer pleasure; Florian, a boy of nine, wrote in the visitors' book, 'I had the best time! Papa fell in the water!' The visit is accurately billed as a discovery walk, and sometimes visitors discover themselves as well as the environment.

'Art, play and nature' – Guillaume's phrase – create very genuine magic here. Bridges, like the door sculptures of

The *Water Staircase* by Michelle Elsair and Jean-Pierre Delettre is an elaborate, multi-faceted sculpture and avant-garde *son et lumière* show.

Jean-Claude Gagnieux, become rites of passage. Taboos are broken: the same artist has created a sign bearing the words 'Listen, you can hear the ocean' which invites you to put an ear to a hanging toilet bowl (a nod to Marcel Duchamp, perhaps?). You hear, amplified by a long pipe, the stream rushing below. A privy-like structure by Guy Jauquères offers peep-holes labelled 'You must not look in these holes', and of course you do. Elsewhere, a hanging drum reveals a display of animal droppings – woodland traces – including mouse pellets left by owls. This is an unsentimental garden which acknowledges prey as part of woodland life and death. Guillaume notes that children often experience nature through their first confrontation with wild animals killing for food, as well as through their first awareness of growing plants and their first attempt at constructing artefacts. For him, these are all part of one and the same natural process.

Guillaume has had plenty of opportunities to observe children. He has two offspring of his own, and for twenty years he taught youngsters with special needs, in particular autistic children. After growing up in Morocco and Senegal, he also found time to work as a trekking guide in the Andes, as a barman, a ski-mender and the inventor of prizewinning computer software. He is now included in the French *Who's Who* under the category 'Atypical'. Le Vallon reflects his broad experience in its appeal to people of all backgrounds and ages. The uphill slope is a comfortable one to walk, even for the more mature visitor, while baby-carriers can be borrowed at the park's entrance.

Guillaume considers himself a 'shower of art', and he has exhibited works by Pierre Soulages, Antoni Tàpies, Andy Goldsworthy, Ernest Pignon-Ernest, Nils-Udo,

At Le Vallon du Villaret, the sculpture *Wolf, Are You There?* by Rachid Aoumari draws the eye up towards the playground of jays and squirrels.

Joachim Mogarra and many more. He advertises in camp-sites as well as museums. At comparable locations, such as the La Vassivière Art Centre in the Limousin, some visitors come to fish and swim and others to look at the land art, but few do both. Le Vallon's artworks invite such active and enjoyable participation that the split between élite and popular publics disappears altogether. The park has already won prizes from both tourist and environmental agencies. Some writers have called it an 'anti-Disney' park, imagining an artisanal David confronting an industrial Goliath. Guillaume notes with pride that his investment-to-visitor ratio is far better than Disney's. Many of his visitors come back over and over again. Entrance is free for children less than a metre tall and for the unemployed.

Signposting poses problems in all new green tourism sites, artistic or otherwise. How to inform the public without intruding on its direct perceptions and experience? Signs are an important pedagogical element at Le Vallon, and they are a model of the genre. Discreet red and yellow owls indicate paths up and back, and riddles appear here and there on tree trunks, much as they do in any initiatory voyage: the answers are to be found in the park's tower.

Augustin Berque, France's foremost landscape philosopher, commends land art for its communion of art and environment, of solitary and social experiences. At Le Vallon du Villaret, everyone can walk alone like English artist Richard Long, enjoying an immediate experience which is 'animal' and individual but which is not anti-social and remains on the human scale Berque so much admires. The last word belongs to Riviera artist Ben, writing in three languages (including Provençal): 'Lo Vallon es very Nice!' And so it is.

Art in the wilderness

Three geological systems meet at Le Villaret – granite, shale and limestone – allowing great diversity in the vegetation: Martagon lilies and orchids, verbascums, vetches and lacy umbellifers, sky-blue columbines, lavender geraniums, wild lettuce, pulmonaria, thyme and bedstraw, varied grasses and ferns all thrive among sorbus, dogwood, beech and birch, spruce and sylvan pine. Everywhere sunlight and dappled shade half hide and half reveal a mask here, a riddle there. Net passages (from the Atelier de Cantagal) let you float through space. The artworks form an integral part of the wilderness setting.

6

PLANETARY
PERSPECTIVES

French gardeners, like those elsewhere, benefit from world-wide exchanges of plants and knowledge, while at the same time fearing invasive species and untested discoveries. But there is optimism: 'The home garden offers a model for world management. If we make use of today's knowledge of plant and soil life and new technologies, we can hope for an optimal and durable partnership with the earth', so wrote French ethnobotanist Pierre Lieutaghi in 1980, long before the full force of globalization became apparent.

Finding the right balance between 'local' and 'global' in France means first of all harmonizing the country's six hundred unique *terroirs* with a strongly centralized national government and the even larger vision of the European Union. What the outside world sometimes perceives as French ecological reluctance is often, in fact, conflict between different levels of government. All groups voice commitment to a quality environment, but discord frequently arises. A case in point is the shocking *Official Catalogue*, or European seed list, which forbids the sale of any unregistered varieties, with draconian conditions and penalties that have crippled small producers of heirloom seed types. Among them is the innovative Terre de Semences, which for years has worked closely with the American Seed Savers' Exchange and suppliers from all

The international garden festival at Chaumont-sur-Loire involves artistic creation as much as botanical expertise and draws on worldwide talent.

over the world – an excellent example of global solidarity for the preservation of local character.

Biodiversity, defined by conservationists in 1992 as 'the totality of genes, species and ecosystems present in any given region', begins at home. In France, farmers, hunters and home gardeners all know their own bit of the countryside intimately, though they often disagree on how best to take care of it. There is, however, a growing sympathy between gardening and a kind of agriculture that is not purely organic but described as 'integrated', respectful of ecological concerns and linked to local growing conditions. This is both progress and a return to tradition: for centuries, French peasants sowed and harvested land according to each small field's special needs and capacities. But modern agribusiness, introduced after the Second World War, led to mechanized mass sowing and harvesting of one crop on all the land on the same day, whether it was ready or not. Today, however, farming, with the aid of technology, is beginning to come full circle. One farmer in the American Midwest beats the competition by analysing his wheat crop with a laptop computer from his tractor as he harvests, so he can profile each plot's needs and potential, as peasants once did intuitively. Peasant lore still survives in France, though today's French farmers also use computers. The luckiest benefit from both their ancestors and the internet, and work with a personal attention that makes them more like gardeners.

From the grass roots up, country gardening in France is becoming more and more linked to community spirit. One movement known as Cultivons la solidarité offers gardening opportunities for the unemployed, packaging produce for delivery to city consumers. One of France's oldest garden-club networks, the Jardiniers de France, now has fifty-three experimental community gardens which provide meals for the homeless. In other cases, ecology is the main motivation. Some young designers, like the Bruel-Delmar Workshop, specialize in community conservation projects, imagining designs closely linked to each site's specific biotope.

The Workshop's gardens at the ethnobotanical research centre Le Prieuré de Salagon and the Conservatoire botanique national de Gap-Charance (both in Haute Provence) draw many visitors every year. Green tourism of this kind provides a major link between each small *terroir* and the outside world, especially as international tourism experts list France as the world's favourite tourist destination. But green tourism is not just for strangers. Home gardeners are opening up their gardens and visiting each other more and more. Remote communities are also learning the value of

Designer Gilles Clément has been the main spokesman in France for planetary gardening, inspired by his experiences creating Le Domaine du Rayol.

gardens in promoting the rural economy. The tiny village of Arlanc in the Massif Central now offers its Jardin pour la Terre, a six-hectare map of the world outlined in gardens, each 'continent' displaying plants that originated on its faraway soil but are now grown in the Auvergne. Arlanc combines local and global viewpoints, entertainment and education in a manner common in public parks all over France. The line between pedagogical and commercial interests is thin, but in the best instances the two work together.

A French pioneer in garden globalization was the Centre Terre Vivante at the Domaine de Raud, set in a remote village of the Alps, and created by the founders of the magazine *Les Quatre saisons du jardinage*. Actively and internationally ecological since the early 1970s, this team now offers workshops in alternative energies and organic gardening drawing on experts from all over the world. Its vision is not 'bucolic and archaic' (words with which environmentalist Alain Roger dismisses many ecologists) but very future-orientated. And its gardens, in which designer Gilles Clément has actively participated, are very beautiful.

In 1999, Clément received the honour of being the first garden designer to organize a national exhibit at the Parc de la Villette in Paris. It was called the 'Planetary Garden'. Interested from his youngest days in both home gardens and biological balances, Clément travelled the world studying plant populations and environments. He feels that gardeners have always aimed at maintaining a harmony between indigenous and introduced species under their care, and that today we must 'push back the garden walls' to extend this vigilance to the entire planet. Gardening is preservation and protection but also discovery, adventure, dream. As humans, ourselves part of the biosphere, we have every right except the right to destroy. Clément has little patience with

While the Rayol gardens re-create worldwide biotopes, the Terrasson gardens aim at universality by evoking international garden archetypes.

Anglo-Saxon 'native plant' purists. Though recognizing the dangers of invasive species, he feels that international mixing is unavoidable. Controls must ensure maximum diversity, not purity of origins. A large section of the Villette exhibit offered models for responsible planetary living for all 'gardeners' living lightly on the earth, promoting sustainable and renewable energies.

Gardeners worldwide will recognize these themes, though the exhibit was as sensuous, playful and poetic as it was didactic. It was green tourism at its best, aiming as much at children as at adults, preserving the past to build the future in the hope that all the world may become a well-tended and productive country garden.

Garden Archetypes from around the World

The Vézère valley in the Dordogne, classified by Unesco as 'The Valley of Man', preserves France's most famous prehistoric sites. At its northern end lies Terrasson, a town of 7,000 inhabitants living from small industry and farming. In 1992 an enterprising mayor, Pierre Delmon, imagining 'a new kind of cultural tourism', held an international competition for a six-hectare public park on the theme 'The Gardens of Humanity'. The winning design had to be worldwide in its scope but also had to enhance the regional setting. Kathryn Gustafson, an American working in Paris, won the commission, along with Anton James of Australia and Philippe Marchand and Frank Neau of France. Her solution to the global/local challenge was to set universal garden archetypes in a design encompassing and orchestrating local 'spirit of place'. Les Jardins de l'Imaginaire opened officially in 1996.

Kathryn Gustafson had hands-on gardening experience as a child and a student, but came to landscape architecture after seven years in the fashion world. After graduating from the École nationale supérieure du paysage in Versailles, she realized many major

At Terrasson, existing woodland was integrated into the new design, with open spaces and broad paths between centres of interest for leisurely discovery.

commissions in France, Britain and the United States, including designs for Shell, Esso and L'Oréal near Paris, the town centre of Evry, a motorway crossroads near Marseilles, greenhouses for the Villette museum in Paris, and, since Terrasson, the Crystal Palace in London, the National Botanic Garden in Wales, and the American Museum of Natural History in New York. She now leads a field of landscape architects which is resolutely cosmopolitan, requiring huge budgets for vast enterprises. The Terrasson project is a rare provincial and rural example, designed on a scale usually reserved for major urban centres.

Elegant minimalism, dynamic movement using water and wind, site sensitivity and technological prowess all characterize Gustafson's work. Terrasson's references to garden universals are interpreted with originality yet are easy to recognize, remaining as sensuous as they are conceptual. One of the best examples is the Parterre Perspective, parallel flowing lines that stretch out like waves on the lower hillside, a mix of blue-flowering nepeta, white roses and beige-plumed grasses. You can discover the detail from within, but from above and below the lines are strong, simple and compelling. Another is the shaded, four-part Elemental Garden, where through the taller tree trunks runs a golden thread of Ariadne – an aluminium ribbon anodized to a gold colour, suspended three metres off the ground by stainless-steel cables hung from protective collars so as not to damage the trees. This alone transforms a static scene into something dynamic, thrusting past echoes into future motion. The effect is breathtaking.

Each archetype is carefully prepared in its approach and siting. A broad path along the hillside offers a first glimpse of a glass 'lake' in the distance. This is the roof of Ian Ritchie's greenhouse, cited in architecture magazines for its advanced technology. From below (on the return lap), it seems to be only a high, rounded wall of local stone held in place by wire netting (the traditional *gabion* method). Inside

is a café, the shop and a collection of citrus plants in pots (the Orangerie motif). Ritchie wrote that he wanted this structure to seem to emerge from the earth, to belong to the earth, to bring the sky down to the earth.

Farther along the path, a lone water geyser comes into view, anticipating the shape of the first in a line of century-old poplars beyond the spectacular water garden. A long narrow canal reflecting the clouds above accompanies this path towards a 'forest' of fountains (agricultural irrigation fixtures), which frame the nineteenth-century farmhouse on the hill rising beyond with more poplars, more geysers.

Gustafson's minimalist but symbolic language of forms can be linked to one major trend of international land art. On site, it requires absolutely pristine upkeep for its various geometries and vistas to achieve maximum effect. These are not, as is often written about this garden, the 'fragments' of postmodern fashion but part of an organically conceived, coherent whole, a beautiful harmony among existing and new elements, stasis and motion, local tradition and the cosmopolitan avant-garde. Traditionally, land art, like landscape architecture, was generally associated either with permanence (built structures meant to last for decades) or decadence (ephemeral creations disappearing in a few hours or less). Plants, when present, were rarely even named. Gardeners missed growth in these conceptions – the time span which moves from seed to flower to fruit.

The public sometimes complains that the gardens at Terrasson are lacking in seasonal change, plant variety and floral display. The design studio's plant lists would suggest otherwise: different parts of the hillside are planted to flower throughout the growing season. The tiered banks

Architect Ian Ritchie's greenhouse has walls of local stone and an amazing glass roof, which from afar looks like a small lake among the trees.

above the water garden, covered entirely with blue and white bloom, contain an impressive array that includes delphiniums, perovskia, salvias, artemesias, violas, tradescantia, meconopsis, phlox, saxifrage and veronicas. And the ratio of flowers to greenery at Terrasson is probably not so different from that common in many traditional public parks. Perhaps the minimalist conception, however well realized, needs time to be accepted in a country setting.

Perhaps also, however, Terrasson, a major model for green tourism as a means of rural renewal, could be more 'user-friendly'. The borders of the water garden, for example, rise behind the fountains and cannot be examined close up. Paths around it peter out as dead-ends. Above all, individual exploration is not permitted, only group tours. Visitors would more likely return to appreciate seasonal variety if they were allowed to explore on their own. Surely both modes could be offered?

Guided visits at Terrasson illustrate another current garden fashion: the linking of spatial itineraries with narrative. For those who wish to listen, this storytelling can bring out symbolism not immediately apparent, making explicit intended references to past traditions and local customs. All new public gardens must face the problem of verbal accompaniment, whether in the form of panels, signs, brochures or live guides, to explain to visitors what they are seeing. But the hillside at Terrasson offers many moods in many weathers and seasons. Those who prefer should be able to write their own private narratives in their own time.

To succeed in its purposes, Terrasson must be accessible to the public in as many ways as possible. The director, Jean-Paul Dumas, has organized a successful annual springtime colloquium called 'The Rake and the Pen', where practical gardeners and theoreticians can meet and exchange insights.

The hillside gardens of Terrasson link wild woodland above and human history below, in the form of the medieval town.

But he has also sponsored an Easter-egg hunt for local children. He is happy that one visitor congratulated him on offering the only public site in the Périgord which smells neither of goose liver nor of flint! All the townsfolk at Terrasson can be proud that the kind of project normally reserved for big cities has settled so harmoniously into the countryside of deepest France. At Terrasson, local initiative has successfully aimed at international recognition, creating a garden where regional character achieves universal meaning.

An itinerary of archetypes

The Sacred Wood at Terrasson offers a myriad of little bells on oak trees, with five cascading streams representing the five great rivers of the world. The shady Pergola leads to the four-part Elemental Garden, planted mainly with azaleas, camelias, cornus and pieris. Up stone steps, the Moss Garden covers stone terracing echoing local ruins. Beyond the 'glass lake', tiers of dark metal benches in grass form the open-air Amphitheatre. Then there is the Water Garden, the suspended Rose Garden, the Parterre Perspective, the Topiary Tunnel and the Fountain Path lined with an iris collection and flowering trees (evodias, amelanchiers and red-buds).

Mediterranean Biotopes from Five Continents

℃

Le Domaine du Rayol sits in a wild Mediterranean valley between two rocky promontories in the Var department, between the eastern Riviera and western Provence. In the 1880s, a lazy little train ran along its dramatic coastline, a failed attempt to attract tourists. Only woodsmen, hunters and perhaps farmers working tiny terraced orchards found their way among Le Rayol's cork oaks and chestnut trees. This was, however, the belle époque, when great cosmopolitan Riviera gardens were being created. In 1909 a banker called Courmes and his young wife bought the land and built a wedding-cake-style hideaway, which became, after the First World War, the imposing Grand Hôtel de la Mer. The couple, meanwhile, had moved to a smaller Art Deco house with a formal garden, also still extant on the eastern edge of the valley. In 1934, facing financial ruin, the banker threw himself into the sea, and his reluctant widow sold the property. Six years later, the famous aviator Henri Potez bought all nineteen hectares of Le Rayol, including the Grand Hôtel, which became the headquarters of his aeronautics company. One ground-floor office housed a financial advisor named Chirac, the father of a

The Central American gardens at Le Domaine du Rayol, while participating in the sequence of global biotopes, preserve traces of the original park.

future French president. Allied landings nearby spared Le Rayol, but a subsequent period of abandonment let nature take over once again. This was its brief century of human occupation, so colourful and typical of Côte d'Azur glamour.

In the 1980s a housing development was proposed, but strong local objections led in 1987 to Le Rayol's purchase by the influential government-sponsored agency the Conservatoire du littoral. The valley first appealed to this essentially conservationist organization as a fragment of 'unspoiled' nature, the dry and rugged local *maquis*. But at the same time, its rich cultural heritage could not be denied. The decision was taken not merely to preserve the past but also to develop the entire area's potential as a new kind of garden. In 1988 Gilles Clément was asked to make a proposal. He was by then already deeply involved in formulating the concept of planetary gardening, the whole earth viewed as a garden with humankind as its caretaker. The existing mix of local vegetation and exotic plants led to the idea of re-creating at Le Rayol landscapes and unique vegetal formations, or 'biomes', from regions around the world with comparable climates to make a global Mediterranean garden. The aim was to study, on the one hand, the specificity of each region's native or endemic plant populations and, on the other, the rich potential for worldwide exchange. Today, the garden has sections inspired by the countrysides of Australia, California, Central America, Chile, China, New Zealand and South Africa.

Walking round the six hectares of garden is not only delightful and instructive, it is different each time. In keeping with his 'moving garden' approach, Clément refused a fixed image to which the plantings would always conform, but preferred a dynamic organization allowing for continuous experimentation and spontaneous growth. He is particularly interested in the age-old rapport between Mediterranean plants and fire which, in many parts of the world, ensures landscape renewal. Unsurprisingly, however, the Conservatoire du littoral has yet to consent to a programmed forest fire.

Visitors enter the garden through the Grand Hôtel. From its vast festooned balcony one can see sunlight glanc-ing off distant islands and also the tree-tops below, massed like waves with brilliantly coloured highlights, intriguing and inviting but basically unreadable from this vantage point.

Each re-created landscape has its own requirements, sometimes needing special technology, and each has its stars. The Australian mallee shows off banksia, eucalyptus, grevillea, acacia (fifty varieties) and callistemon species, as well as kangaroo paws (*Anigozanthos*). The subtle colours of the New Zealand grasslands set off olearias, tea-trees (*Leptospermum*), phormiums, and a deep shady valley of tree ferns kept moist with artificial mist. The carex lawn has had to be replaced by Texan *Stipa tenuifolia*, but the overall appearance is unaltered. The South African landscape, the *fynbos*, has the densest concentration of species per square metre, and some of the most colourful contributions, including amaryllis, carissa, leonotis, watsonia, polygala, pelargoniums and the

'King' protea (*Protea cynaroides*), which Clément admires so much that he used it as a symbol in the mosaic he made with his own hands beside the grand pergola. Chile brings its zigzag bamboos (*Chusquea* sp.), alstroemerias, various nasturtiums (*Tropaeolum* sp.), monkey-puzzle trees (*Araucaria*) and cactus candles. The Canary Islands feature echiums and convolvulus, while the Californian garden includes carpenteria, romneya and ceanothus. The Central American section best recalls the picturesque belle époque design, circling around Washingtonia palms and colourful shrubby sages. A special rockery was created for the Mexican cactus garden, but this poses real problems for weeding since no chemicals are allowed. By the beach, an underwater garden is just beginning to develop with protected beds of sea urchins.

Between and around these managed plantings extend open and wooded stretches of local vegetation, often sweeps of wild-flower meadow. There are surprises: a wild-flower seed mix from a French supplier proved to be full of South African natives. Inevitably, plants self-sow. The gardeners monitor this evidence of successful acclimatization to avoid takeovers by plant thugs. The South African katrou acacia, the Canary Island echiums and a yellow oxalis present here for two centuries have been allowed some leeway among the local cistus, terebinths, broom and laurustinus. In Clément's planetary garden, human intervention and management always aim at promoting maximum diversity.

To create Le Rayol's biomes, Clément and some of the park's botanists explored the wildest regions of all the five continents (at their own expense). In 1997, Clément published *Thomas and the Traveller: Sketch of a Planetary Garden*, a collection of imaginary poetic and philosophical exchanges

The balcony view at Le Rayol shows tree-tops massed like waves, the design unreadable from above. This is a garden to be discovered from within.

The cactus garden at Le Domaine du Rayol, much appreciated by visitors, poses problems for weeding without chemicals.

between a stay-at-home gardener and a wanderer. The two men discuss such topics as 'horizon', 'grass', 'erosion', 'city', 'shade', 'fire', 'legend' and, finally, 'garden'. The book inspired Clément's 'Planetary Garden' exhibit at the Parc de la Villette in Paris in 1999. Maturing during the same period of reflection, Le Rayol is perhaps Clément's most successful living example of a planetary garden, 'a system', says his character Thomas, 'without limits of life, without boundaries, nourished by the dreams of gardeners and constantly remodelled by the changing conditions of nature'.

Planetary exchanges

Le Domaine du Rayol re-creates biomes or ecosystems with similar climates from all over the world. Its rich bio-diversity is carefully managed, full of colour, texture, scent and discovery, and never the same twice. Its designer, Gilles Clément, defines the contemporary garden as a privileged terrain for experimentation, rejecting architecture as the only defining principle, and turning, instead, to dynamic biological process. He claims that planetary exchanges both enrich and threaten us, and asks 'Can a garden orientate the debate?' Le Rayol is his attempt at such a garden.

An International Garden Festival in the Loire

Every summer since 1992 a great garden festival has been held at the Château de Chaumont in the Loire valley – not in the formal park but around the old farm buildings at the top of the nearby hill. Thirty bell-shaped plots of about 250 square metres each display, over a four-month period, the most avant-garde imaginings of 'creators, architects, designers and botanists' from all over the world. Each year has its special theme: 'Is Technology Poetically Correct?' in 1996; 'Waterworks' in 1997 and 1998; and 'Kitchen Gardens' in 1999. One hundred and fifty thousand visitors came in 1998 to discover what the young generation can do with a deliberately limited budget but boundless imagination. With no clients to satisfy, the results are often wacky and wonderful displays of technical prowess and off-beat humour, a kind of garden gallery where the plastic arts, engineering, ecology, innovative design and plantsmanship all intermingle.

The Chaumont Festival is an offshoot of the Conservatoire international des parcs et jardins et du paysage, the brainchild of Jean-Paul Pigeat. Co-author as early as 1970 of the influential book *Diseases of the Environment*, Pigeat devoted some twenty years to a vast variety of projects involving nature and art, city and country, social welfare and creativity. He describes himself as a man with a gift for finding talent and getting things started. Chaumont's festival began as an exhibit for the Pompidou Centre in Paris but, nearly strangled by red tape, it was saved *in extremis* by the Région Centre-Val de Loire and Jack Lang, the then minister of culture. Today a permanent foundation, Chaumont is eighty-five per cent self-financed, the rest coming as subsidies from the local and regional governments. It may soon start to make a profit, thanks to its newly founded advisory design business, which has already been employed both locally and internationally: in the Gloriette Park in the nearby city of Tours, for example, and in two symbolic peace gardens for Bethlehem and Nazareth.

The summer festival offers scope for creative young people from all over the world. Many of the 1999 kitchen gardens mixed colour and food in unusual ways. Scottish designers Nigel Buchan, Frazer McNaughton and Lumir Soukoup imagined a 'Tartan Garden' of purple cabbage, blue leeks and red sage, surrounded by a gatherers' wild garden with

The international garden festival at Chaumont-sur-Loire presents brilliant new design ideas in the grounds of a Renaissance château.

'La Bidouille', which mimicked *grandpère's* allotment, was one of many potagers at Chaumont 1999 to mix tradition and outrageous invention.

pines, birch, cardoons and hazelnuts. A Portuguese student at Chaumont designed special Azulejos tiles to present the ingredients for the typically Portuguese dish pork *à l'alentejana*. A monastery garden by American monk Brother Victor Antoine d'Avila Latourrette even provided recipes. Jean-Luc Danneyrolles's Provençal heirloom vegetable garden offered a cornucopia of multicoloured delights. 'India Song' by veterans Patrick Blanc and Eric Ossart included a rainbow array of vegetables evoking the spring

equinox festival when people throw coloured powder and water over each other. 'La Bidouille' humorously imitated *grandpère's* allotment garden, complete with a rusty bicycle; festival visitors feel free to picnic in this plot.

Also in 1999, California-inspired 'raised bed' vegetable plantings were especially commended for family gardening by journalist Jean-Paul Collaert. At Chaumont they were set in elegant galvanized-tin tubs designed by internationally celebrated architect Jean-Paul Wilmotte. Americans will remember that Californian promoters of this method twenty years ago cited as their model nineteenth-century French intensive market gardening. What better example could there be of fruitful international exchange?

As laid out by Belgian designer Jacques Wirtz in 1992, the experimental plots are surrounded by five-foot-high beech hedging. This imposes a standardizing frame and usually a single point of entry, a dominant angle of vision, which some designers are at great pains to deflect and multiply. More and more designers let you walk around inside, and even encourage you to make things happen. The plots also vary in their terrain, sometimes involving slopes and terracing, sometimes closely backed by neighbouring exhibits. Only two Japanese exhibits have so far 'borrowed' the surrounding landscape – the turrets of the Renaissance château.

Today, the festival offers special activities for children, including treasure hunts and a scarecrow workshop, a participatory exhibit where they can get soaking wet on hot summer days. Many of these activities can easily be copied for public parks. There is also a restaurant, which chef François-Xavier Bogard (who trained with Michel Guérard)

'India Song' by Eric Ossart and Patrick Blanc alludes to a spring equinox festival where people cover each other with coloured powder and water.

prefers to call 'inventive' rather than 'gastronomic', and also a light, good, fast and cheap pasta bar. Both feature organic produce grown by the Blois chapter of Les Jardins de Cocagne, a movement promoting the re-employment of the jobless. Spices come from all over the world, but the herbs are grown at Chaumont. Every October, the Conservatoire de Chaumont participates in the national Semaine du Goût. And all year round there is a public library, colloquiums, training sessions with diplomas offered in conjunction with the nearby University of Tours, and workshops for students who help set up the festival in the spring. Germans, Canadians, Japanese, Italians, Portuguese and Spaniards now attend courses there.

Sometimes, the Chaumont style is deliberately provocative – a proliferation of dwarfs, for instance, or an exhibit featuring a flooded and mouldy camping truck. Humour and wit have been encouraged from the outset in design selection. So has technical virtuosity, which perhaps benefits professionals more than the public at large. But much of the show leaves you breathless with delight. One can be inspired just by the variety of surfacing materials: pine needles in the bamboo tunnel; olive stones in the 'Gazpacho Garden'; seaweed, mussel shells and pine cones in the 'Tartan Garden'. Chaumont is a giant playground, the most up-market example of green tourism, and for everyone a land of dreams. It is also an experimental laboratory on a planetary scale.

Global gardening

Famous American architects participated in Chaumont's early years, among them Peter Walker, George Hargreaves and Richard Haag. Today, many designers from poorer countries take part, illustrating, for example, watering techniques used by Moroccan peasants, or a Bangladeshi garden of vegetables rich in vitamin A, sponsored by the Helen Keller Foundation. Japanese artist Suzuki created at Chaumont his only garden outside Japan, and experts from Hangzu in China designed an octagonal garden symbolizing the place of man in the cosmos. French botanist Patrick Blanc, famous for his 'Living Wall' gardens, brought back treasures from Chile for the festival, but also found good exotics in the Chinese district of Paris.

'Haute couture'

Some observers feel that Chaumont offers the 'haute couture' of French garden design, creations that perhaps few people would actually 'wear' but which everyone can admire and enjoy as a spectator. But some of its inventions are now imitated all over the country. One example is woven live-willow fencing. At Chaumont, this technique first appeared as a set of curtains rising from clouds of artificial mist, imagined by English designers David and Judy Drew, and looking like cool, minimalist sculpture until enlivened by children running delightedly around inside.

USEFUL ADDRESSES

THE AUTHOR
E ljones@wanadoo.fr
W www.gardeninprovence/louisaJones

**GARDENS AND PARKS FEATURED IN THE BOOK
WHICH ARE OPEN TO THE PUBLIC**

INTRODUCTION

Conservatoire botanique de Brest
52 allée du Bot, 29200 Brest
T 02 98 41 88 95 F 02 98 41 57 21 E cbn-brest@infini.fr

Office national des forêts
2 avenue de Saint-Mandé, 75570 Paris Cedex 12
T 01 40 19 58 40 F 01 40 19 78 95 W www.onf.fr

Conservatoire du littoral
36 quai d'Austerlitz, 75013 Paris T 01 44 06 89 00
F 01 45 83 60 45 W www.conservatoire-du-littoral.fr

Conservatoire international des parcs et jardins et
du paysage de Chaumont-sur-Loire
Ferme du Château, 41150 Chaumont-sur-Loire
T 02 54 20 99 22 F 02 54 20 99 24
E cipjp.documentation@wanadoo.fr
W www.chaumont-jardins.com

Ecomusée d'Ungersheim
68190 Ungersheim T 03 89 74 44 74 F 03 89 74 44 65

Les Jardins de l'Albarède
24250 Saint Cybranet
T/F 05 53 28 38 91 E jardins.albarede@wanadoo.fr
(Owners: Serge & Brigitte Lapouge)

CHAPTER 1

Le Jardin de la Pomme d'Ambre
Via Aurélia, la Tour de Mare, 83600 Fréjus
T 04 94 53 25 47 F 04 94 52 95 50
E info@gardeninprovence.com
W www.gardeninprovence.com/frnicole.html

Le Jardin de la Galérie Doudou Bayol
quartier Plantier Major, 13210 Saint-Rémy
T 04 90 92 11 97

Château de Mongenan
16 rue Mongenan, 33640 Portets
T 05 56 67 08 11 F 05 56 67 23 88
(Owner: Florence Mothe)

Le Jardin de la fondation Claude-Monet
27620 Giverny T 02 32 51 28 21 F 02 32 51 54 18
W www.fondation-monet.com

CHAPTER 2

Les Jardins de Bellevue
76850 Beaumont-le-Hareng
T 02 35 33 31 37 F 02 35 33 29 44

Les Jardins des retours
Corderie royale, Centre International de la Mer
BP 50108 17300 Rochefort
T 05 46 87 59 84 F 05 46 99 02 16
E contact@corderie-royale.com
W www.corderie-royale.com (Designer: Bernard Lassus)

Le Bois des Moutiers
route de l'Eglise, Varengeville-sur-Mer
T 02 35 85 10 01 F 02 35 85 46 98
(Owner: Antoine Bouchayer-Mallet)

Le Vastérival
76119 Sainte-Marguerite-sur-Mer
T 02 35 85 12 05
(Owner: Princess Greta Sturdza)

L'Arboretum des Grandes Bruyères
Les Tourelles, 45450 Ingrannes
T 02 38 57 12 61 F 02 38 57 11 79
(Owner: Les Parcs et Jardins de France)

Château de Momas
64230 Lescar
T 05 59 77 14 71 E momas@chateauxcountry.com
(Owner : Marie-Joseph Teillard)

Villa Noailles
boulevard Guy de Maupassant, 06130 Grasse
Grasse tourist office T 04 93 36 66 66
F 04 93 36 86 36

Kerdalo
22220 Trédarzec
T 02 96 92 35 94 W www.bouture.com/kerdalo.htm
(Creator: Prince Wolkonsky; owner: Isabelle Vaughan)

L'Arboretum de la Fosse
41800 Montoire-sur-le-Loir
T 02 54 85 38 63 F 02 54 85 20 39
(Owner: Jacques Gérard)

Château de Courson
42 boulevard de la Tour Maubourg, 75007 Paris
T 01 45 55 41 74 F 01 47 05 10 91
E coursondom@aol.com W www.coursondom.com
(Owners: Patrice & Hélène Fustier)

Le Jardin d'Anne-Marie
2 rue du 8 mai 1945, 91510 Lardy
T/F 60 82 30 63
(Owners: M & Mme Yonn Grivaz-Ginies)

Plantarium de Gaujacq
40330 Gaujacq
T 05 58 89 24 22 F 05 58 89 06 62
E pepibotagaujacq@thoby.com
W www.thoby.fr

Pépinières Côté Sud des Landes
RN 12, 40230 St Geours de Maremne
T/F 05 58 57 33 30
(Owner: Philippe Labbe)

Pépinières Planbuisson
rue Montaigne, 24480 Le Buisson de Cadouin
T/ F 05 53 22 01 03
(Owner: Michel Bonfils)

Michel Lumen
Les Coutets, 24100 Creysse
T 05 53 57 62 15 F 05 53 38 54 88
E lumenviva@aol.com

L'Arboretum de la Sedelle
Villejoint, 23160 Crozant
T 05 55 89 83 84
(Owners: M & Mme Philippe Wanty)

Les Jardins d'Agapanthe
76850 Grigneuseville
T 02 35 33 32 05
(Owner: Alexandre Thomas)

L'Arboretum du Pré des Culands
45130 Meung-sur-Loire
T 02 38 63 10 49 F 02 38 63 10 49
(Owner: Pierre Paris)

Parc floral de la Source
Mairie d'Orléans, Département Espaces verts
1 place de l'Étape, 45040 Orléans Cedex 1
T 02 38 79 26 F 02 38 79 20 23
W www.parcfloral-lasource.fr

La Verderonne
9 rue du Château,
60140 Verderon par Liancourt
T 03 44 73 10 67

CHAPTER 3

Le Jardin gothique du Musée de
l'Oeuvre Notre-Dame
3, place du Château, 67000 Strasbourg
T 03 88 52 50 00

Les Jardins de Limoges
Tourist office T 05 55 34 46 87
Pierre Lagedamon T 05 55 58 28 44

USEFUL ADDRESSES

Château d'Yvoire
74140 Yvoire
T 04 50 72 88 80 F 04 50 72 90 80
E mail@jardin5sens.net
W www.jardin5sens.net
(Owners: M & Mme d'Yvoire)

Château de la Guyonnière
79420 Beaulieu-sous-Parthenay
T 05 49 64 22 99
(Owner: Valérianne Dugois)

Château du Colombier
Mondalazac, 12330 Salles la Sources
T 05 65 74 99 79 F 05 65 74 99 78
E colombier@thoiry.tm.fr W www.thoiry.tm.fr
(Owners: Paul & Annabelle de la Panouse)

Château de Chamerolles
45170 Chilleurs aux Bois
T 02 38 39 84 66 F 02 38 32 90 91

Château d'Ainay-le-Vieil
18200 Ainay-le-Vieil
T 02 48 63 50 67
(Owner: Marie-Sol de la Tour d'Auvergne)

Le Jardin romain
71110 Varennes-L'Arconce
T 03 85 25 92 05 F 03 85 25 89 00
(Creator: Monique Lafon; owner: Association
du Jardin des Cinq Sens)

Domaine médiéval des Champs
Le Villard, 48230 Chanac
T 04 66 48 25 00
(Director: Anne Trémolet de Villers)

Les Routes de la Lavande
2 avenue de Venterol 26110 NYONS
T 04.75.26.65.91 F 04.75.26.32.67
E info@routes-lavande.co
W www.routes-lavande.com

Château de Villandry
37510 Villandry
T 02 47 50 02 09 F 02 47 50 12 85
W www.chateauvillandry.com
(Owner: Henry Carvallo)

Château de Miromesnil
76550 Tourville-sur-Arques
T/F 02 35 85 02 80

Château de Galleville
76560 Doudeville
T 02 35 96 54 65

Château de Bosmelet
76720 Auffay
T 02 35 32 81 07 F 02 35 32 84 62
W www.chateau-de-bosmelet.fr

Château de la Bourdaisière
Conservatoire nationale de la tomate
37270 Montlouis
T 02 47 45 16 31 F 02 47 45 09 11
W www.chateaulabourdaisiere.com

Château de Saint-Loup-sur-Thouet
79600 Saint-Loup-Lamairé
T 05 49 64 81 73 F 05 49 64 82 06

Château de Saint-Jean-de-Beauregard
91940 Saint-Jean-de-Beauregard
T 01 60 12 00 01 F 01 60 12 56 31
E info@domsaintjeanbeauregard.com
W www.domsaintjeanbeauregard.com
(Owners: M & Mme de Curel)

Le Jardin musée de Limeuil
24510 Limeuil
T 05 53 63 32 06
(Owners: Michel & Véronique Guignard)

Le Prieuré de Salagon
04300 Mane
T 04 92 75 70 50 F 04 92 75 70 51
E Musee.salagon@wanadoo.fr
W www.musee-de-salagon.com
or www.cg04.fr
(Owner: Conseil général)

Les Jardins des Paradis
place du Théron, 81170 Cordes-sur-Ciel
T 01 55 63 56 29 77 & 06 03 10 05 84
W www.cordes-sur-ciel.org

CHAPTER 4

Les Jardins de l'Alchimiste
Mas de la Brune, 13810 Eygalières
T 04 90 95 90 77 F 04 90 95 99 21
E contact@jardin-alchimiste.com
W www.jardin-alchimiste.com
(Owner: Marie de Larouzière)

Les Jardins de Cadiot
Camp Redon, 24370 Carlux
T/F 05 53 29 81 05
(Owners: Bernard & Anne-Marie Decottignies)

Jardin Eric Borja
Les Clermonts, 26600 Beaumont-Monteux
T/F 04 75 07 32 77

Les Jardins de Labyrinthus
71 rue de la Presle, 37000 Tours
T 02 47 42 63 62 F 02 47 42 65 64
W www.labyrinthus.com

Château de Hautefort
24390 Hautefort
T 05 53 50 51 23 F 05 53 50 55 03

Manoir d'Eyrignac
24590 Salignac-Eyvigues
T 05 53 28 80 10 F 05 53 30 39 89
W www.eyrignac.com
(owner Patrick Sermadiras)

Château de Marqueyssac
24220 Vezac
T 05 53 31 30 00 F 05 53 28 94 94

Jardin de Monsieur Mausset
le Bas Beaumont, 87260 Saint-Paul
T 05 55 09 76 10

Le Jardin Plume
Le Thil, 76116 Auzouville-sur-Ry
T 02 35 23 00 01 E lejardinplume@wanadoo.fr
(Owners: Patrick & Sylvie Quibel)

Le Prieuré de Notre-Dame d'Orsan
18170 Maisonnais
T 02 48 56 27 50 W www.prieuredorsan.com

Château de la Ballue
35560 Bazouges-la-Pérouse
T 02 99 97 47 86

CHAPTER 5

Le Jardin d'Elie
Association de sauvegarde, Nicole Manéra (president),
20 chemin de Sabatery, 83136 La Roquebrussane
T 04 94 86 83 (at meal times only)

La Roseraie de Berty
07110 Largentière
T 04 75 88 30 56 F 04 75 88 36 93
W www.roseraie-de-berty.fr.st
(Owners: Eléonore Cruse)

Le Vallon du Villaret
Le Hameau du Villaret, Allenc, 48190 Bagnol les Bains
T 04 66 47 62 89 F 04 66 47 63 83
W www.capnemo.fr/vallon
(Owner Guillaume Sonnet)

Jean Kling
La Nouvelle Agence
T 01 43 25 85 60 F 01 43 25 47 98

Le Jardin de Berchigrange
88640 Grange-sur-Volonge
T 03 29 51 47 19 F 03 29 57 57 97
W www.berchigranges.com
(Owners: Monique & René Dronet)

Les Jardins de Sauveterre
Laboutant, 23200 Moutier-Malcard
T/F 555 80 60 24 W www.chez.com/sauveterre
(Owners: Jacques Girardeau & Colette Vérot)

Pépinières Filippi
RN 113, 34140 Meze
T 467 43 88 69 F 467 43 84 59
E olivier.filippi@wanadoo.fr W www.jardin-sec.com
(Owners: Olivier & Clara Filippi)

Pépinières de Vaugines
route de Cadenet, 84160 Vaugines
T/F 490 77 13 80
(Owner: Gérard Weiner)

Les Jardins de la Forge
Villejoint, 23160 Crozant
T 05 55 89 82 59
(Owners: Christian Allaert & Jacques Sautet)

Centre d'art et du paysage de la Vassivière
87120 Beaumont du Lac
T 05 55 69 27 27 F 05 55 69 29 31
E centre.d-art.vassiviere@wanadoo.fr

La Fondation Stahly
Centre d'art et de sculpture, chemin de la Verrière,
84110 le Haut du Crestet, Vaison la Romaine
T 04 90 36 34 85 F 04 90 36 36 20

Pépinières André Eve
45300 Pithiviers le Vieil
T 02 38 30 01 30 F 02 38 30 71 65

CHAPTER 6

Terre des Semences/Association Kokopelli
Oasis, 131 impasse des Palmiers, 30100 Alès
T 04 66 30 64 91 F 04 66 30 61 21
E kokopelli.semences@wanadoo.fr
W www.kokopelli.asso.fr
(Owner: Dominique Guillet)

Festival des Jardins de Chaumont-sur-Loire
Conservatoire international des parcs
et jardins et du paysage de Chaumont-sur-Loire,
Ferme du Château, 41150 Chaumont-sur-Loire
T 02 54 20 99 22 F 02 54 20 99 24
E cipjp.documentation@wanadoo.fr
W www.chaumont-jardins.com

Le Domaine du Rayol
Avenue des Belges, 83820 Le Rayol-Canadel
T 04 94 05 32 50 F 04 94 05 32 51
W www.domaineidurayol.org

**Jardins 'Cultivons la solidarité' and other similar
associations**, see W www.jardinons.com

Jardiniers de France
40 route d'Aulnoy, BP 559,
59308 Valenciennes Cedex
T 03 27 46 37 50 F 03 27 29 08 12

Conservatoire botanique national de Gap-Charance
Domaine de Charance, 05000 Gap
T 04 92 51 21 79 F 04 93 51 94 58

Le Jardin pour la Terre
Terre Neyre, 63220 Arlanc
T 04 73 95 00 71 F 04 73 95 78 31
E jardin-terre.arlanc@wanadoo.fr

Centre Terre Vivante
Domaine de Raud, BP 20, 38711 Mens, Isère
T 04 76 34 80 80 F 04 76 34 84 02
E infos@terrevivante.org W www.terrevivante.org

Les Jardins de l'Imaginaire
24120 Terrasson
T 05 53 50 30 66 F 05 53 50 46 76
(Director: Jean-Paul Dumas)

PROFESSIONAL DESIGNERS FEATURED

Alain Richert T 01 43 57 16 77 F 01 43 57 06 09
Gilles Clément T 01 43 48 61 33 F 01 43 48 93 23
Camille Muller T 01 43 67 46 95 F 01 40 09 04 79
Dominique Lafourcade
    T 04 90 92 10 14 F 04 90 92 49 72
Arnaud Maurières & Eric Ossart
    T 02 54 55 06 37 E ossart-maurières@wanadoo.fr
Michel Semini T 04 90 72 38 50 F 90 72 38 52
Louis Benech T 01 44 05 00 21 F 01 44 05 95 65
Jacques & Peter Wirtz T (32) 3 680 13 22
    F (32) 3 680 13 23 E info@wirtznv.be W www.wirtznv.be
Erwan Tymen T 02 97 65 99 76 F 02 97 65 03 46
Atelier de Paysages Bruel-Delmar
    T 01 47 00 00 51 F 01 47 00 13 51
Kathryn Gustafson E KatGustaf@aol.com

**HOW TO FIND OUT MORE
ABOUT FRENCH GARDENS**

Association des parcs botaniques de France (APBF)
15 bis rue de Marignan, 75008
T/F 01 42 56 26 07 (Tuesday afternoons only)
W http://apbf.asso.free.fr

**Association des parcs et jardins
de France en région centre**
14 bd Rocheplatte, 45000 Orléans
T 02 38 77 10 64 F 02 38 53 42 20
W www.jardins-de-france.com

Château de Courson
42 boulevard de la Tour Maubourg, 75007 Paris
T 01 45 55 41 74 F 01 47 05 10 91
E coursondom@aol.com
W www.coursondom.com

Comité national pour le fleurissement de la France
Arche de la Défense Paroi Sud,
92055 Paris la Défense Cedex 04
T 01 40 81 37 82 F 01 47 73 71 01

La Gazette des jardins
23 avenue du Parc Ribiony, 06200 Nice
T 04 93 96 16 13 F 04 92 15 00 61
E redaction@gazettedesjardins.com
W www.gazettedesjardins.com

Parcs et jardins de France
45450 Ingrannes
T 02 38 57 12 61 F 02 38 57 11 79
E blr@club-internet.fr
W www.parcsdefrance.org

Société nationale d'horticulture de France (SNHF)
84 rue de Grenelle, 75007 Paris
T 01 44 39 78 78 F 01 45 44 99 57
W www.snhf.org

FURTHER WEBSITES

www.parcs-jardins.com
www.plantes-et-jardins.com
www.jardinez.com
www.colvir.net/prof/laurent.deschamps/france/jardins
www.monum.fr/m_monumvert
www.chateauxetjardins.com
http://perso.club-internet.fr/phengels
    in partnership with www.garden-open.com
www.parcsetjardins.fr

BIBLIOGRAPHY

Abbs, Barbara, *French Gardens: A Guide*, Lewes, 1994
Albertazzi, Liliana (ed.), *Différentes natures: Visions de l'art
    contemporain*, catalogue of exhibition at La Défense,
    Galérie Art 4 et Galérie de l'Esplanade, Paris, 1993
Arboireau, Nicole, *Les Jardins de grand-mère*,
    Aix-en-Provence, 1998
L'Architecture d'Aujourdhui: Paysage,
    April 1989, no. 262